Down Under from Devon

Henry Godfrey 1824–1882

Down Under from Devon

Rosemary Petheram

The Pentland Press Limited
Edinburgh · Cambridge · Durham

© Rosemary Petheram 1993

First published in 1993 by
The Pentland Press Ltd.
1 Hutton Close
South Church
Bishop Auckland
Durham

ISBN   1   85821   005   4

Typeset by Elite Typesetting Techniques, Southampton.
Printed and bound by Antony Rowe Ltd., Chippenham.

To my sons, John and Brian,
and my sister, Norah, as a tribute
to our mutual forebear.

DOWN UNDER FROM DEVON

Letters written by Henry Godfrey,
a pioneer settler in Australia from 1843,
compiled with the addition of background information
by his great-granddaughter
Rosemary Petheram

Contents

Illustrations

Introduction

In copying the letters written by my great-grandfather, Henry Godfrey, when he was on the voyage from Plymouth to Australia in 1843 and during part of the time he was living there as a pioneer settler, I have made a point of altering as little as possible. The phraseology, spelling and punctuation, the use of emphasis and of capitals are all reproduced exactly as written in these letters, which have survived in the family for almost a hundred and fifty years. They give some insight into the character of the man and illustrate facets of the age in which he lived. The inclusion of personal details relating to members of his family help to add human touches about the individuals concerned. Thus nothing he wrote in these letters to his relatives at home has been omitted, though for the sake of clarity I have introduced paragraphs and have isolated the dates used in the form of a diary describing the events he recorded.

I have obtained the information for the accompanying background material from various sources. Some facts I have deduced from inferences given in the letters, but nothing is wholly guess-work. Certain details have been verified by reference to text books and I have found almost all the places mentioned on a large scale map of Victoria.

Compiling this account has been rather like solving a jig-saw puzzle – fitting together fragments of the past from the available family records – a task which proved laborious and time-consuming, but one I have found altogether fascinating and ultimating rewarding.

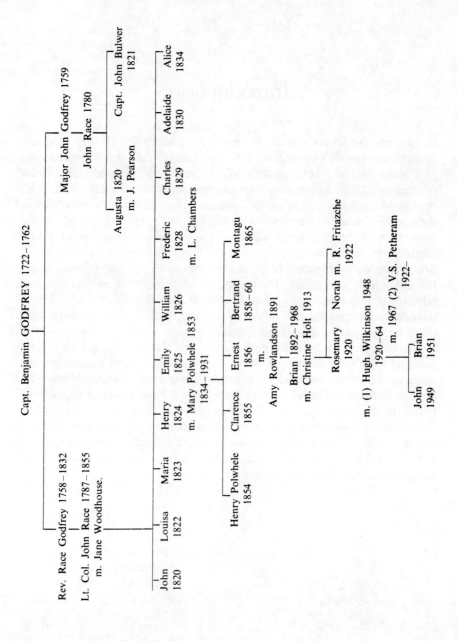

Capt. Benjamin GODFREY 1722–1762

Rev. Race Godfrey 1758–1832

Major John Godfrey 1759

Lt. Col. John Race 1787–1855
m. Jane Woodhouse.

John Race 1780

Augusta 1820
m. J. Pearson

Capt. John Bulwer
1821

John
1820

Louisa
1822

Maria
1823

Henry
1824

Emily
1825

William
1826

Frederic
1828

Charles
1829

Adelaide
1830

Alice
1834

m. Mary Polwhele 1853
1834–1931

m. L. Chambers

Henry Polwhele
1854

Clarence
1855

Ernest
1856

Bertrand
1858–60

Montagu
1865

Amy Rowlandson 1891
m.

Brian 1892–1968
m. Christine Holt 1913

Rosemary
1920

Norah m. R. Fritazche
1922

m. (1) Hugh Wilkinson 1948
1920–64

m. 1967 (2) V.S. Petheram
1922–

John
1949

Brian
1951

xiv

1

The Remembered Past

To have a great-grandmother living was something quite unusual. At any rate Mary Godrey's great-grandchildren thought so. None of their contemporaries could claim to have a relative of this calibre, so the two small girls felt proud to be able to tell people their Great-grandma was still alive. She was their father's grandmother – the mother of their elderly Grandpa; thus they realised she must be very old indeed. In fact she had already turned ninety when the elder child first became aware of her existence in the middle 'twenties. Everyone in the family hoped she would live to be a hundred and receive a telegram from the King, but sadly this was not to be. She died in 1931, four years short of her century.

It was usually towards the end of the summer that the children and their mother used to spend a week or two staying with their paternal grandparents on the outskirts of Exmouth. The weather in early September was nearly always fine and sunny, enabling them to spend part of each day down by the sea, not returning until they had eaten the picnic tea they had brought with them. By then the little girls were tired, having spent hours playing on the beach, making sand castles, hunting for shrimps and crabs in the rock pools and splashing about in the water. It was a long walk back to Littleham Cross, all uphill, too. Thus Great-grandma's house afforded a welcome haven of rest half-way back from the sea-front and the old lady was sure to be at home after five o'clock. Earlier in the afternoon she used to go for a drive in her carriage – an open landau drawn by an old horse, driven by a coachman correspondingly advanced in years. The horse clip-clopped at a leisurely pace along the promenade or down the shady country lanes – and in those days the lanes around Exmouth were quite unspoilt and virtually free of traffic. The old lady wore a Queen Alexandra-style toque with a spotted veil over her face and a feather boa draped elegantly round her shoulders, secured by a jet chain. Later on, after the horse had died, she was obliged to take her daily outing in a motor car, insisting that the chauffeur should drive no faster than she had been accustomed to travelling in the carriage, which he must have found a tiresome imposition.

The children were glad to reach the wide white gate with the name Ferniehurst on it. Their mother rang the bell beside the glass-fronted porch and they were admitted by a parlour-maid neatly dressed in a black frock and crisp white cap and apron. They stepped into the remarkably spacious entrance hall, which was quite as large as any ordinary drawing room and always seemed nice and cool after the glare of the sun outside. A staircase with a massive balustrade curved upwards on the right. There was a red cord attached to the wall so as to provide a secure hand-hold for the old lady when she went upstairs. The lofty ceiling towered above the upper floor and the bedrooms opened onto a balcony surrounding two sides of the hall. On the left of the front door was the morning room. The children rarely entered it, but if the door was ajar they got a glimpse of fine Regency furniture decorated with golden scrolls. All the articles in the room were highly polished and looked just as if they were on display in a museum.

The next door on that side opened into the breakfast room and they sometimes went in to take a peep at the picture of Great-grandma when she was young. It was not until many years later when their father had inherited all the family portraits that the elder girl realised she had always looked at the wrong picture.

"That – " her mother had said with an expansive gesture of her hand, "That is what your Great-grandma was like when she was a young woman."

The child thought she was pointing to the picture of a damsel with long loose hair, the neckline of whose frock was quite immodestly low. She appeared to be washing her feet in a stream. The figure of a young man with incipient side-whiskers and a simpering smile was seen approaching from behind some bushes. Was he supposed to represent Great-grandpa in his youth? The lady's careless dress seemed rather shocking and it was hard to imagine Great-grandma posing for her portrait like that. The pair of pictures in heavy gilded frames hanging over the sideboard on the adjoining wall attracted little attention. One was of a handsome woman with dark brooding eyes and a long straight nose. Her hair was parted in the middle and swept upwards at the sides in wide wings. She was wearing a blue frock, the square neckline trimmed with white, and heavy gold beads adorned her shapely neck. The accompanying portrait of her husband was still less interesting. For one thing it was so dark that only the eyes, brow and nose were at all clearly visible; the thick brown hair and hugely luxuriant beard merged with the gloomy background, obscuring all detail of the lower part of the face. He gave the impression of having been a stern and dignified character who inspired small grounds for curiosity or interest.

That Mary Godfrey had in some way been connected with Australia, her

Mary Godfrey (née Polwhele) 1835–1931

great-grandchildren came to accept at quite an early age, though all further facts were obscure. They knew Australia to be a continent on the other side of the world where eucalyptus trees grew, the home of kangaroos and koala bears, the place where the natives used boomerangs for hunting. Indeed boomerangs did have some real relevance for the children because there were several of these strange curved weapons arranged decoratively on the far wall of the entrance hall along with a couple of spears and a narrow oval shield, thus giving credence to the Australian connection. They were also told that the name of the house, Ferniehurst, was the same as a place near where their great-grandparents had lived in that southern continent. But what of the woman herself whom these children of the 'twenties were destined to remember as someone they had been privileged to have known in the flesh?

They had to get tidy before going into the drawingroom to see the old lady. They washed their hands in the downstairs cloakroom and their mother brushed their long straight hair, re-tying the ribbon bows they wore. She reminded them to speak clearly, as the old lady was rather deaf, and to be sure to say "Good afternoon" on entering the room. Sand was emptied out of their sandals. It would never do to soil the spotless floors in that grand house. When they were ready they followed their mother along the dark passage leading out of the far end of the hall, their feet sinking into the deep pile of the carpet, making no noise. There was a baize-covered door at the end of this passage leading into the kitchen regions and the servants' quarters, but the children never penetrated into this part of the house. Their mother knocked on the door on the left and a frail voice bade them enter. They went in.

Mary Godfrey was seated in a low armchair facing the fireplace. She looked a shrivelled little figure, but there was certainly something dignified and commanding about her aristocratic features. At the age of six or seven the elder child was convinced the old lady sitting there must be a queen – either Queen Victoria or Queen Elizabeth. The confusion concerning her possible identity was partially due to the light brown wig she wore. Not for one moment was it suspected to be a wig, of course – though it did seem rather odd that such an old person was not yet white-haired. Queen Victoria had been talked about in the children's hearing and they knew she belonged to a comparatively recent period in history, but Great-grandma didn't look in the least like the pictures they had seen of her. She wasn't fat and dumpy for one thing – and then there was that sandy-coloured hair. Pictures of Queen Elizabeth showed her to have had hair rather like that as well as the aquiline features and the heavy eyelids. Yet surely Queen Elizabeth had lived hundreds of years ago and Great-grandma couldn't possibly be as old as all that? Later on it came as quite a shock to find out about the wig. One day the sandy-brown coiffeur was seen to be tilted slightly askew. Thin strands of white hair protruded from beneath it – the hair of a very old woman who evidently had very little of it left.

She smiled, showing her false teeth, and extended a thin blue-veined hand to draw the children towards her. The knobbly joints of her fingers were heavy with jewelled rings. Her skin, when her cheek was dutifully kissed, felt soft and crêpey like an old kid glove and she smelt of eau-de-Cologne. It is a pity nothing remains in living memory of what she said on these occasions. She could have told about her childhood in the Cornish rectory overlooking a picturesque creek beside which stood the little church of St. Anthony-in-Menaccan where her father, William Polwhele, officiated and where her grandfather, the historian and writer Richard Polwhele, had held the living before him. She could have described her feelings during the long voyage to Australia in a sailing ship soon after her marriage to Henry Godfrey when she was only eighteen. Her husband, ten years older, had by then already established a successful sheep station in the outback. She might have talked about her life as a pioneer's wife in the bush far from any other settlers. Of black men and kangaroos, strange plants and insects and poisonous snakes. Surely, too, of adventures, loneliness and tragedy. Her fourth son had died there in infancy. She could have told also of the good times she must have had with her children, each of whom owned a pony. An oil painting shows Ernest, aged about six, astride a little garron while his elder brother holds the bridle of another horse and their bearded father stands between them wearing light-coloured breeches and highly polished riding boots. A fierce-looking Aborigine carrying a tall spear and a shield stands at one side. They are grouped outside a wooden cabin constructed of transverse planks. The date on the back of the frame is 1863 and there is a note to the effect that the black man was known by the name of Prince Charley.

No, unfortunately the old lady did not talk about the past, or if she did her great-grandchildren were too young to remember what she said. She was a little deaf and rather crippled with rheumatism, but her sight was good and her intellect quite unimpaired. Over ninety, she tended to be rather crochetty at times, she was always exacting and particular, often imperious and perverse – sometimes positively dogmatic and autocratic – but never senile. Her library subscription provided her with the most recently published books. She read *The Times* and *Punch*, while the weekly issue of the *Illustrated London News* she always passed on to her grandson's family.

Henry Godfrey at Boort with his sons Ernest (on the pony) and Polwhele. The Aborigine was a member of the Loddon tribe; he was known by the name of Charley.

Beside the chair where the old lady sat there was a long, low cane-topped stool on which her books and papers lay. A settee with a tall back, covered in shadow-printed cretonne, stood at right-angles to the fireplace. Here the white cat was often curled up asleep. Like his mistress this cat was very old. People used to wonder whether he would outlive her, but the cat was the first to die though he reached the great age of twenty-two.

While their mother was talking to the old lady the children were able to admire the many beautiful objects in that spacious drawingroom. There were all kinds of china ornaments on the wide marble mantelshelf and elsewhere in the room. Especially attractive in the children's eyes was a sort of bracket attached to the opposite wall near the door into the conservatory. It represented a nymph seated in a grotto from the roof of which hung icicles or stalactites, all beautifully tinted in pink and white.

Less attractive, but perhaps still more fascinating, was the large oriental china figure squatting on a nearby table. Of Chinese or Japanese origin, it represented a portly individual clad in gaudily painted robes. When gently touched, the head nodded to and fro in a life-like manner and with every forward movement the tongue shot out between the parted lips. As the movements ceased the tip of the tongue remained visible protruding from one side of that leering mouth, while the slanting eyes seemed to look inscrutable and self-satisfied in the plump china face.

On the wall beside the door into the room there was an oil painting of a sailing ship passing a towering iceberg. The ship, its sails billowing, looked to be running before the wind through choppy green water touched with crests of spray. The children were told their great-grandfather had travelled home from Australia in that ship before he was married. This picture was to assume greater significance in the years to come.

Mary Godfrey seldom rose from her chair while the visitors were present. On one occasion when she walked across the room to pick the purple blossoms from a clematis plant in the conservatory to give to the children, she moved very slowly, and shuffled along leaning heavily on her ebony stick with its blunt silver ferrule and ivory handle, her long skirts almost touching the floor. She uttered rhythmic grunts as she went, probably from habit rather than from pain. Her shoulders were bowed and her dress made a soft frou-frou sound as she walked.

When the time came to leave, the children were expected to kiss their Great-grandma again as she sat with her feet resting on a footstool facing the fireplace. Sometimes she would lift the hem of her skirt to reveal a deep purple petticoat with a flounce around the bottom and from a pocket concealed in the frill she would take out a quaint little purse. It was long and narrow, embroidered with black and silver beads, and there was a tassel at one end. To open it she slid down an encircling ring, exposing a narrow slit, and shook out a few coins into the palm of her hand. Each child was given a piece of silver, usually a shilling, but on rare occasions it was a florin – and that was real wealth! The little girls would thank her politely and kiss the withered cheek as they quietly withdrew to leave her with her memories.

In January 1931 Mary Godfrey had passed her ninety-sixth birthday. Throughout her long life she had enjoyed remarkably good health. She had always continued to eat exactly what happened to take her fancy and scorned any suggestion that it might be wiser to moderate the rich diet she enjoyed. At ninety-six she could still get around her house and go out for a drive, and her mind remained active. The idea of ill-health was utterly repugnant to her. Had she been confined to bed for any length of time she would undoubtedly have proved an extremely difficult patient, so when the news came in May that she was unwell the family was distinctly apprehensive. What course would her illness take?

Her son Ernest was in the habit of visiting his mother every day, going down the road from Littleham Cross to Douglas Avenue on his bicycle. He was a stickler for punctuality and his routine never varied. The two children came with their mother every Saturday to have lunch with the grandparents in Exmouth. On 23rd May their Grandpa was late for the meal that was all ready to be served, but which on no account could be started without him. He had gone to see his mother during the morning as usual, though now she had been in bed three or four days. Amy, his wife, began to fidget. Ernest was never late. Then came the sound of the front door opening and Ernest Godfrey came into the drawing room where the family was waiting, not pausing in the hall to take off his coat. He passed his hand across his eyes wearily. Suddenly he looked older and smaller than in the past. "She's gone!" was all he said.

"Oh Ernie . . ." Amy's blue-veined hand touched the black velvet ribbon she wore round her throat. The children said nothing. This was the first time death had affected them at all closely. The elder girl was ten years old. She thought she ought to cry, but no tears came. She just felt numb. So Great-grandma was dead, failing to reach her century by only four years. This was the end of an era.

The imprint of the old lady's personality was to remain indelibly printed on the mind of that child who through her had glimpsed the opulence of the Victorian age. Happily for Mary Godfrey, she did not live to experience the financial slump of 1932 which could well have had an adverse effect upon her way of life. To the end she was able to live in the manner to which she had become accustomed after her return from Australia where her husband had done so well. Her life had been a full and satisfying one.

There can have been little physical resemblance between the very old lady the two small girls knew during their early childhood and the young woman who had accompanied her husband to a new land half a world away nearly eighty years before when she had left behind everything familiar to her up to that time. Yet they were one and the same – and the fact that her great-grandchildren could remember visiting Mary Godfrey at the end of her life was to provide a remarkable link with the past, not only with persons long dead and a vanished age, but also, as it was to turn out, with the actual spot where the family had lived and where their name is perpetuated in a tiny corner of Australia.

2

Gone – Not Forgotten

So far it has been seen how Mary Godfrey is remembered as an unforget-table character by her great-granddaughters in the twentieth century, but what of her husband who died so many years before she did, even before the birth of their father in 1892? To his descendants in later generations Henry Godfrey might well have been regarded as a shadowy figure identified only by the portrait in which he appears a serious, indeed a rather forbidding sort of individual. But fortunately enough information exists to help build up a more realistic picture of that stern-looking Victorian gentleman with the luxuriant beard and reveal him, in his younger days at any rate, to have been a most enterprising and discerning person who possessed a nice sense of humour.

A large metal deed box containing documents relating to members of the family has been handed down since the time of Henry's father, John Race Godfrey, or even earlier. Among the piles of certificates, photographs, newspaper cuttings, pedigrees and diaries there are a number of letters which were evidently considered worth preserving. The most interesting of these are the letters written by Henry Godfrey to various members of his family during his first voyage to Australia in 1843 and those written when he was living in the outback before he returned home to marry and bring his young bride to the homestead he had established there. The last of these is dated 1849.

The originals of the letters written in the course of the voyage have been lost, but they were copied out on foolscap sheets by his father and they certainly give a vivid picture of life on board a sailing ship in the early years of Queen Victoria's reign. Transcribed with a quill pen in ink that has faded, the writing is not easy to read, in spite of the cursive script being neat and even. It took many hours of careful scrutiny to decipher and type out these letters, the task being made still more difficult by having to contend with the now happily obsolete style of the first s in a word containing two adjoining being made to resemble the letter f. However the effort was amply rewarded because now, thanks to this correspondence of his, Henry has to some extent been brought back to life.

Lieutenant Colonel John Race Godfrey was born in Bath in the year 1787, the second son of Major John Godfrey, 11th Dragoons, J.P. for Somerset. In 1820 he married Jane Octavia Woodhouse whose eldest brother was Richard Woodhouse, the close friend of John Keats who accompanied the poet to Italy. All but one of John and Jane's ten children were born in India where their father served for thirty-six years, being awarded a medal with two bars in the First Burmese War. Henry, the second son, was born at Madras on 4th June 1824. Upon retirement John Race settled with his large family at 5 Pennsylvania Park, Exeter – later acquiring the lease of Northernhay House, an imposing mansion situated close to the remains of the ancient Roman walls which once surrounded the city and overlooking the grimmer walls of Exeter Prison down in the valley. Mary Godfrey told her sons how she heard that the servants in the home of her parents-in-law liked to look out of the attic windows or even climb up onto the roof so as to watch executions take place in the prison yard below. Northernhay House was demolished early this century, but 5 Pennsylvania Park still exists.

The family was a united one, the chidren being devoted to their parents whom they held in the deepest esteem and affection, while an unusually close rapport existed between the brothers and sisters – perhaps not really surprising, since the first seven of them had been born on consecutive years.

In common with many young people of their day who came from well-to-do homes, the Godfrey boys and girls led a lively social life and were able to provide their own amusements at home by means of their not inconsiderable musical talents. It was then considered normal, indeed obligatory, to learn to play some kind of instrument – thus they were able to combine their various accomplishments to present evening entertainments featuring songs and music from the 'cello, violin and piano. Henry is reputed to have had a fine tenor voice and to have continued to sing well on into his middle years.

Sketching, too, was considered a usual pastime – not always with outstanding results, of course, but in Henry's case his drawings and paintings show considerable artistic skill and great delicacy of execution. Little can he have imagined that some of them would one day bring him posthumous fame.

The Godfrey boys were educated at Exeter Grammar School and Henry left there in 1841 when he was seventeen. By that time he had evidently decided he would go to Australia and make a career for himself sheep farming in the regions now being developed by many pioneer settlers from Great Britain. With this end in view he spent the next year in South Wales near Boventon and Lantivitt Major in Glamorgan at the farm of a Mr Powell whom he described in a letter home some years later as his "friend and mentor". Here he learnt all about farm management as well as the basic skills needed in running a farm – the care of sheep and cattle, the sowing and harvesting of crops, tree-felling and carpentry – to fit him for the demanding life he expected to lead in the wilds of Australia where success would depend on his initiative, perseverance and relevant knowledge.

At this time his younger brothers had not yet completed their education at the Grammar School. Henry's letters show him to have been a mature and confident young man who had plainly benefited from the good education he had received. He had a fluent command of English and was well grounded in Latin. In those days any interest in natural history was directed principally towards the destruction rather than the preservation of wild species. Most young men learnt to shoot with the object of being able to participate in the "sport" of killing birds and animals. The ability to use firearms was certainly something Henry would need in the Australian outback where it was customary to possess a shotgun for the purposes of culling, of obtaining food and no doubt, in certain circumstances, for self-protection. Yet Henry does not seem to have shared his father's interest in nature study to quite the same extent as his younger brother Frederic, who made repeated references in his surviving journals to the birds and plants he came across in Australia. Some of the birds he shot in order to preserve the skins so that his father might add them to the collection he had accumulated during his life in India. Colonel Godfrey had a large and valuable collection of foreign birds stuffed and mounted which was presented after his death, by his widow, to the city museum in Bath.

Coming as he did from a conventionally religious background Henry was familiar with the contents of the Bible in which he believed implicitly and it is clear from his letters that his faith meant a great deal to him. It was a source of support and comfort when facing the problems and difficulties he encountered in the kind of life he had chosen to lead.

In a period when the railways were still in their infancy in England and as yet non-existent in most other parts of the world, it was necessary for travellers to go about the country on horseback or by carriage and in stage coaches; thus most men could ride and knew how to manage horses. This was just as well in Henry's case since he was to find he had to travel vast distances on horseback or driving a trap when he was settled in the remote part of Victoria where he eventually took up residence.

It is not known what prompted this eighteen-year-old boy to decide to take the momentous step of leaving the home where he was so happy and parting from the family he loved so dearly in order to sail away to the other side of the world. The region where he chose ultimately to settle and make a living was at that time largely unexplored. The continent had been occupied by white settlers in the easterly coastal areas only during the past fifty-five years or so, and the interior was as yet undeveloped and uninhabited by white men. The penal settlements in Van Dieman's Land and at Botany Bay had tended to give these parts of the Antipodes a rather unsavoury reputation, but as the nineteenth century advanced it was realised there was great potential for the development of the land for farming – both for stock rearing and the production of cereals – as well as for the exploitation of its mineral wealth.

There is nothing to suggest it was his parents who persuaded Henry that he should go so far away from home. The decision to emigrate was clearly his own idea, though his father did give him substantial financial backing. Motivated by the spirit of adventure and the desire to prove himself capable of achieving success in a wholly new environment, he faced the prospect of what lay ahead with determination and excitement, though not without some degree of trepidation, as was only natural. There is certainly little hint of homesickness in the early letters he addressed to those far away in Exeter whom he held so dear.

The voyage to Australia in the eighteen-forties was under any circumstances bound to be long, lasting up to three months or more depending on the vagaries of the winds and currents; it was bound to be tedious and not without some degree of discomfort, while there was also always the risk of encountering storms or being becalmed for lengthy spells, but young Henry Godfrey was fortunate in being able to travel under the best conditions available at that time. Not for him the overcrowded and unhygienic state of affairs endured by the immigrant steerage passengers who were forced to put up with cramped quarters and monotonous or inadequate food; still worse was the miserable plight of the convicts shipped out to face a life involving wretchedness, privation and brutality, in some cases for no greater crime than petty theft.

Henry's father could afford for him to have the best accommodation available on board ship. He had a cabin to himself and enjoyed the exclusive privileges accorded to the small number of other First Class passengers – sitting at the Captain's table and partaking of a high standard of food and drink. It will be seen he had no cause for complaint about the meals which seemed, indeed, to have been rather more than adequate. He was not behindhand in expressing his gratitude to his father for enabling him to travel in comfort but, as it happened, the first letter he wrote on board was to Maria, the sister nearest to him in age.

Nevertheless it was his father who kept all the correspondence received by members of the family from Henry in the course of his voyage and who painstakingly copied out everything that was written, including the meticulous details of latitude and longitude recorded as the ship sailed southwards. Before copying the letter addressed to Maria, which had doubtless been eagerly read by every member of the family, John Race Godfrey wrote:

'My dear boy's first letter from Sea on his outward Voyage to Van Dieman's Land. He left Exeter on the 3rd. March and sailed on the 7th. March 1843.'

3

The Correspondence

The first letter Henry wrote on board ship was to his sister Maria who was less than a year older than he was. For this reason their relationship had always been very close. At this time, as he approached his nineteenth birthday, she had not yet reached twenty.

Passengers on outward-bound sailing ships relied on encountering ships returning home in order to send the letters written on board back to England. This must have been quite a chancy business, depending largely upon the state of the winds and currents, there being no means of prearranged communication. The sight of another vessel after days of sailing in the seemingly boundless ocean was certainly a welcome diversion and the two were able to exchange information by means of a universal system of flag signals.

Henry was fortunate in having some congenial fellow passengers on the *Duke of Roxburgh*, particularly, it would seem, in the Nixon family and Archdeacon Marriott. His comments in the course of his correspondence give a good idea of their characters and dispositions. Bishop Nixon of Tasmania was returning to Hobart with his wife and daughters. The two elder girls were permitted to take their meals at the Captain's table together with Miss Wills, their governess, but little Mary – the youngest – must have been provided for elsewhere in the care of a nurse-maid.

An interesting passenger was John Helder Wedge, a pioneer to Van Dieman's Land where he had acquired considerable property and he was one of the first white settlers in the Port Phillip area of Australia. He and the Bishop enjoyed sketching, an interest they shared with Henry who took the liberty of copying from their sketch books when unable to produce original drawings of certain subjects he was anxious to record.

Of course seasickness was an unavoidable accompaniment to life on a sailing ship, a state of affairs aggravated by the pitching and tossing of the vessel which was something wholly unfamiliar to those who had never experienced it before. However, in due course everyone became accustomed to the movement and it will be seen that substantial meals were enjoyed without any distressing sequel.

Henry mentions the comfort he obtained from a Bible given him by his
Aunt Ann. She was his mother's elder sister, the fifth of the fifteen children
born to the wife of Richard Woodhouse, senior. She died giving birth to the
last one which did not survive her. Ann's eldest brother, Richard, was a
friend of John Keats.

Gus, mentioned at the end of this letter, was Augusta Godfrey, a second
cousin of Henry's. Her father was John Race Godfrey, a Naval Com-
mander, who lived with his family in Dartmouth – hence the young man's
pleasure at learning Miss Wills had visited a place familiar to him.

On board ship.
Duke of Roxburgh.
Monday 9th. of March 1843

My dearest Maria,

I have commenced this letter to you but do not know when we shall meet
a homeward bound vessel, however I will just mention a few circumstances
that have happened since my dear Father and Uncle left me, and then the
rest of this letter will be in the form of a Diary – not that there is much to be
said for events occurring at sea, for one day, and its constituent incidents, is
very like the one that preceeded it.

Well – on Tuesday the 7th. the anchor being up, away we went –
however, before we left I stood on the Poop to see the very last of the Boat
that bore away from me the ties of Parental care on earth – but I felt that I
was much strengthened and comforted when I needed it most, by the
Almighty hand of Providence – in that although I had lost sight of my
earthly Parent for a season I had a Father in Heaven who promised to hear
the Prayers of all those who call upon his name and who alone could afford
true comfort and joy to the drooping mind.

The Bishop and Mrs. Nixon also watched the boat out of sight as their
dear relatives were on it as well; and after they had left Mrs. Nixon came
and gave me a hearty shake of the hand and remarked how brightly the sun
was shining upon us.

A short time after we had sailed, it being about dinner time – we sat down
at table intending to commit great havoc on the roast Beef etc. but I was not
seated two minutes after having taken some soup before I jumped up from
the table with the soup in my mouth! rushed down below and of course was
what you may term seasick. Up I came again and saw some three or four
more who had seated themselves with good intentions of remaining – but
the flesh was weak – they had vacated their seats. I went below and came up

again three or four times resolved not to give in, but it was no go. I was forced to go to bed. I got up to breakfast on Wednesday Morning – but did not *sit out* the breakfast time, but mark me, I was not *singular*, others followed my good example, even the Lord Bishop! and his Archdeacon was the worst of us all.

Nothing particular on Wednesday. The Bishop being sufficiently recovered read Prayers to us in the Evening. After tea I got hold of Mr. Wedge, and was getting very kind information out of him which he freely gave. He is a very large land owner in Van Diemans Land. He advised me to go to Port Phillip as he said all *good* ground in the Island is occupied. Told me a great many adventures etc. he had met with among the natives, Bushrangers &c. He was the second person that ever landed at Port Phillip.

Today Thursday the 9th. all of us getting rather the better of our sea sickness. I could eat my breakfast this morning but my head is rather giddy as the composition of this will shew, and my hand very weak as the writing will prove. I must leave off for today. Bye the bye before I close I must mention that Miss Wills and myself had a long and interesting chat about Dartmouth – she was there part of this summer. The children are not such *un*interesting objects as Mrs. Woodcock described them. I like them very much. Mrs. Nixon seems a very superior person. I cannot write more, good bye.

Sunday Morning 12th. I have not had, dearest Maria, any thing of interest to write you that has occurred since I left off, but as there is a homeward bound ship in view I hasten to finish this in case it may be sent on board.

I will briefly say that we are all pretty well over our sea sickness – Mrs. Nixon has been a great sufferer. Our sermon this morning was beautifully impressive and most touching in the extreme. The Bishop gave a beautiful sermon, almost extempore, and I played the old 100th. Bedford, and Morning Hymn to the crew, all joining in the praise. One of the sailors after the Sermon said to me "*He hits very hard, Sir.*" He dilated upon the all presence and omniscience of God most eloquently and afterwards about *swearing* and the use of God's name in vain and in fact if I had time I could give you the heads of the Sermon pretty well for it is pretty deeply rooted.

Upon the whole I anticipate a very pleasant Voyage and we have as yet a wonderously prosperous one. We are about 43.32 North. 15 degrees West.

Remember me most kindly to all friends. Give my best love and duty to my Father who has done more than his duty towards his children who ought to be and I think are *more* than grateful for his paternal affection and care. I pray for all of you Morning and Evening. Good bye, love to my dearest and best of Mothers and each and all brothers and sisters, dear relatives and friends.

I suppose Vivian has taken Gus away from you. I cannot at present think of any more for I am rather flurried (so to say). The Bishop reads Morning and Evening. Tell Aunt Ann her Bible is my best companion, comforter and friend. The Bishop's text was from Genesis 16 and 17.

[No signature]

The next letter written on board covers the period from March 13th. to April 11th. During these four weeks the *Duke of Roxburgh* had reached the equator.

The sight of another ship never failed to cause great interest and excitement. A system of flag signals deployed when two vessels were close enough for the symbols to be clearly seen enabled them to communicate in quite a satisfactory manner, though of course this method lacked the advantages of radio contact which was not to come until very many years later.

Henry was fortunate that his father could afford for him to have a comfortable cabin to himself – though in some respects the service seemed not to have been all that might have been expected and it must have been most distressing to discover bugs in the cane mesh beneath the mattress. Their unwelcome attentions obliged him to sleep on a day-bed in spite of using turpentine to try and keep their numbers in check. He decorated his cabin with familiar scenes from home, fastening the pictures to the wall with wafers – these were small adhesive discs used for sealing letters. He had brought his own reading lamp with him. In this connection he refers to the wick as the "cotton". The Bull's eye was the term used for the port-hole.

It would seem Henry's younger brother Willie was expected to join him overseas in the near future. As it happened William was not the next member of the family to make the long journey to Australia. It was Frederic, the seventh of the ten children, who joined Henry in the outback.

Evidently Bishop Nixon was acquainted with Sir Thomas Acland of Killerton near Exeter who supplied him with fresh butter and bacon from the home farm to take on the voyage. One wonders how it was kept in good condition with the onset of the hot weather as they neared the equator.

Henry had certainly never crossed the line before, so his excuse made so as to avoid the traditional rites meted out to all initiates was wholly spurious. Why was he not prepared to join in the fun?

At the end of this letter a note was added by Mrs. Nixon expressing her gratitude for the interest Henry took in her children. Of course it was natural that he would have had plenty of ideas for amusing them and would enjoy their company as he came from a family in which there were six brothers and sisters younger than himself.

On board ship.
Duke of Roxburgh.
Monday 13th. March 1843

My dearest Father,

You may easily imagine what pleasure it gave me to have been able to send a letter home by the opportunity that offered itself yesterday (Sunday) and also that I had previously commenced it so that with the addition of the last day's news I sent home a diary of events up to the time of meeting the homeward bound, as the plan succeeded so will I now follow it up, hoping, tho' *not expecting* to meet with another homeward bound shortly. The vessel that carried our letters (for almost every passenger hastened to scribble a few lines) was the "Mandane" from Singapore. I certainly did long to jump into the boat as it left our vessel.

Did any at home succeed in finding out our advancement by the Latitude and Longitude I sent? On this day of writing I have not yet been on board *one* week yet it seems like one year since I left *dulce domum*. This morning we saw in the distance a vessel coming exactly in the opposite course to our own, however when it had passed us some distance it tacked round and was following exactly on the same course. We had mistaken it for a homeward bound, but it according to *my* idea was coming up to us fast. The Captain said No, that we were leaving her behind. After having come up from my cabin in about two hours she was almost up with us – I had such a laugh against him. We held communication with her by the flags for some time. She was the "Sylph" from London to Barbados, the conversation kept up between us was very new and therefore interesting to me. One of the Mates who had sailed in her before said it would be a wonder if we left any vessel behind us, evidently showing that he did not think her one of the *fastest* of her day!

The Steward certainly has *as yet* done all I have asked him but he has a very unpleasing incivil way of speaking. I cannot say much for him. As for a Cabin boy I have seen no such person, but I make my own bed, get water and empty it after washing and as I shall have to do it by and bye I do not grumble at it on board ship where one has so much leisure time. My boots the Steward gets cleaned, but as for blacking brushes I have not given him any yet, so I am a gainer. Finally as respects the Cabin it is (thanks to you) as comfortable as it can be and as I should wish it. The Lamp burns well, but one ought to speak of its merits after two months trial instead of a week as I have not yet changed the first cotton, I have it about a quarter of an hour every night. The wash basin has been *once* rubbed bright and shall be continued *once* a week. Tell Willie that his valued Drawing of Pennsylvania is the *first* and *most* pleasing sight that meets my eye when it wakes out of sleep, for it is placed at the end of my Bed, just where the light from the *Bulls eye* shines upon it, and before I rise I indulge in a ten minute stare at it thinking of each member of my family at No. 5 and then each respective inmate of the remaining five houses *invicera*. Below it is wafered the print of the Breakwater and again below that the Barbican Pool at Plymouth. Of the comforts and contents of my cabin "*Dat est.*"

The Bishop reads prayers to us every Morning at half-past eight and after them we sit down for breakfast which on board ship is more like a dinner than a breakfast for meat hot and cold of all sorts is on table and we all ply a pretty good knife and fork, although I have not yet got the *ravenous* appetite that I was to have by all accounts. Dinner is also a very sumptuous meal, a great variety and everything nice. We have very good pale Ale and Porter, Port, Sherry, Claret, – Champagne on Sundays and birthdays – and sweet wine. The water is not very good, but Mr. Wedge having a filter on board has offered to filter it for me when I like to send it in.

Lat. 3. 16. Lon. 20. Thursday April 6th. Mr. Wedge shewed me a *very curious* implement, something between a Pistol Gun and a Blunderbus, it throws twelve slugs at one discharge, and sends them horizantally so as to sweep down a group of men at one shot. A famous thing to clear a mob. It is a patent of Wilkinsons in London, damage £50! He said it was given him by one of his neighbours at Launceston when he went to survey Port Phillip and he said he would carry it in his belt with a dozen cartridges. Another advantage is that you can load it ten or twelve times a minute. He advised me upon my observing that I should hide my pistols under my coat or so on, not to do so, but to make all display of fire arms. He said they are more apt to fear you.

We are and have been enjoying fresh butter! even to the line! thanks to the Bishop to whom Sir Thos. Acland gave 3 or 4 jars so that we are eating Killerton Butter and Bacon also.

The stem of my nipple screw has got loose in the handle and I cannot pull out the nipples with my own, – "ergo" the first parcel that is next sent to me may contain a nipple screw like T, a tuning hammer only all steel.

I sleep every night on the folding sofa as the bugs torment me so in bed and I think they were not in the ship but in the Rattan of my bed, for I killed swarms of them in the holes where the cane is driven in. Spirits of Turpentine I used. There is a doctor on board so I can have any medicine at pleasure. I get up generally when I hear the first bucket of water thrown on the Poop about 5 o'clock, sometimes at Mr. Donford's watch at 4. He has given me three or four shower baths already. I walk the poop barefoot in a shirt and those Payjamahs that Augusta made, they are most delightful things. Sometimes I go and sit at the main top.

Mind Willie's boots are not very high in the heel, or else have two or three pair of thin shoes – boots are hot this weather – however I do not wear stockings in them. Cool trowsers that do not need washing are useful. I have but two Pair and those old ones. Waistcoats I do not wear. White Jackets are comfortable.

Today April 7th. I wish General Boles many happy returns of his birthday. One omission of some consequence was a common Violincello Bow to spare my beauty.

Saturday April 8th. Quite a holyday as shaving and ducking took place although we had not crossed the line because next week is Passion week. I got off giving anything or even getting a ducking as I pleaded having crossed the line before. The Bishop gave me £2. It is altogether a very curious custom. The sailors collected only £3.15. I brought my Violincello upon the Poop for the first time, it being a fine Moonlight still evening. Lat.3.2. Long – You see we have been going backwards seven miles.

Sunday 9th. At about six in the Morning the Captn. and myself hooked a shark, but he had not got the barb of the hook far enough in his mouth so he got away. Every body else save the Archdeacon was slumbering. A Barracuda was caught by the sailors and we had him for breakfast. At 7 o'clock a regular fine shower. I stood in my payjamas to have a washing.

The Bishop gave out that the service would be every day of Passion week, and Sacrament administered next Sunday. I hope to communicate.

Today Monday 10th. A ship in sight. Will she speak to us? I have attacked my Raspberry Vinegar, I wish I had more of it, it is so grateful. The Thermr. has been higher than 80. Service performed.

Tuesday Morning 11th. The early bird catches the worm. The Archdeacon and myself being *as usual* up early saw a ship and seeing her on homeward bound, composedly sit down to finish our epistles. I had a bath this morning. At the Cape we shall be in about a month from thence I shall write to some of you.

Mr. Wedge pays much attention to Miss Wills, the initial letter the same –

that looks well. Do not mention my remarks but *in your own circle*.

Mr. & Mrs. Batchelor came from Londoun Place, Bristow Road – so we chat together about that part of the world. Yesterday Lat. 2.38. Long. 20.44. Today not yet taken. I must finish this with remembrances to all the Boles, Powells and love to all relatives near and dear, love and kisses to brothers and sisters and accept the same my dear Father, from your affecte. and dutiful

Henry Godfrey.
The ship is fast approaching.
Goodbye.

Mrs. Nixon added the following note:

My dear Sir,

As perhaps your son may be too modest to tell you himself I have asked for the letter he has just been directing as I am sure you will like to hear how much we are indebted to him for leading our services in our Sunday Psalmody for unfortunately few of us can boast much of a voice. His Violincello adds considerably to the harmony. I am happy to tell you that we all appear to be passing the time very cheerfully, we all seem to have different occupations and amusements – and it would be difficult to imagine a party living in greater peace or more entire harmony. My little ones are greatly indebted to your son who is most kind in assisting to amuse them, and as for little Mary I believe she prefers going to Mr. Dodfrey to any one else.

Believe me,
Yours faithfully,
Anna M. Nixon.

While writing to his father in the form of a diary of events on board ship Henry began a letter to his mother on the same lines, finding enough to say without any repetition.

He described a splendid comet seen from the ship on 17th March which was still visible a week later when the Canary Isles had been passed. This was to become known as the Great Comet of 1843. A contemporary illustration shows it travelling diagonally below the constellation of Orion, the tremendously long tail cleaving the sky in a line as straight as if it were drawn with a ruler. It is believed this comet is not likely to reappear for upwards of a thousand years. If another comet was sighted in 1811 it was certainly not seen by Henry Godfrey who was born thirteen years after this date, so we must take this reference – with the double exclamation points – to be his little joke. On the other hand he might well have seen Hayley's Comet which appeared in 1833 when he was nine years old and he may simply have made an error in writing down the date – or else his father transcribed it wrongly when copying out the letters which now exist in the elder man's handwriting.

Henry was glad to have the opportunity to experiment with his musical talents, finding ample time on board to compose and to practise his 'cello. Another diversion was the presence of the Nixon children. He got on well with them and found they were nice little girls in spite of what a mutual friend had evidently said about them before he left England. He was, of course, used to associating with children, having two young sisters himself.

Rough weather led to water coming in through the port-holes and the general humidity caused considerable damage to all metal objects in the cabins. He was obliged to spend many hours removing rust from the barrel of his gun. However as the ship neared the equator the thermometer recorded much higher temperatures, making it necessary to wear light clothing, while a single blanket was adequate at night.

In this letter he included further advice in the event of his brother William making a sea voyage and he expressed his dislike of tobacco smoke. Later in life he was to change his views and he did occasionally smoke a pipe himself.

On 1st April he remembered his little sister Adelaide's twelfth birthday. His wish for her to have a long and happy life was to be fulfilled. She married Brigadier General Sir Charles Stewart, had four children, and died in her eightieth year.

Duke of Roxburgh.
Friday 24 March 1843

I may be able to write sufficient, my dearest Mother, for a letter to you as well as my Father, since I find no chance of a vessel is likely to offer itself for some time I must try back (to use hunting phraseology) and narrate a few circumstances that I have not mentioned in my Father's letter. Nothing of interest on 16th except the Archdeacon's illness and ergo his interesting eulogy on the occasion.

17th. At half past six in the Evening a fine Comet was visible with an *outrageously uncommonly* long tail, from my faint reminiscence of the one in 1811!! I should come to the conclusion that this one was a fine sight. I wonder the Pocket books did not make mention of it. Did you see or hear anything of it?

18th. Nothing but contrary winds and long faces. A day with a contrary wind is like (only on a larger scale) a Sunday at home with pelting rain.

Sunday 19th. was a very rough day so the service and our peroration was transferred to a cuddy below. The Bishop read all the service as the Archdeacon had not yet recovered – he gave an excellent discourse on the subject of the converted Jailor asking "Sir, what shall I do to be saved? – Believe in the Lord Jesus etc." and in the evening he preached extempore from 12 Matth. 30 & 31 verses, and explained them most fully, also referring us to and explaining the parallel passage in 6 Heb. 4.5.6. verses. His flow of language is most beautiful and delivery very impressive. We sing three Psalms every Sunday morning, and one in the evening. I am the Organist in ordinary to the Lord Bishop of Tasmania!! How important a station.

20th. For the first time put my powers of musical composition to the test and the consequence was the production of a Chant!! of its merits I am not the judge, but I will venture to thoroughly condemn it, and perhaps will try another in the hopes of improvement. I have however given it a place in my valued Manuscript book of Chants. I shall christen it the Roxburgh Chant.

The Bishop read aloud this evening a part of Shakespeare's King John very well indeed.

We were last night all anxiety to see Madeira but it was too dark and foggy so we passed it unseen. Thirteen days to Madeira rather slow work but we have such contrary winds. The air is very mild but we have not yet altered our clothing.

The Bishop's children are not as bad as Mrs. Woodcock described them, one is a great pet of mine, Mary – three of the small fry are rather like our weather, squally at times – I do not like that sort of music so when they begin I leave them to it.

All our live number on board amount to 69 souls, one cow & calf, a Goat and three Dogs and some live Partridges which Mr. Wedge is endeavouring to introduce to Van Diemans Land. There are 36 Passengers altogether. I will name the Cuddy Table crew. The Lord Bishop, his Lady and Miss Wills the Governess, the Archdeacon, Revd. & Mrs. Batchelor, Mr. Lewis (a native of Van Diemans Land) Mr. Wedge one of the early settlers who gives us many interesting events of his life – Mr. Pritchard (a nondescript) quite the joke of the Cuddy – Mr. Maurice the Surgeon – Captain Collard, Mr.

Donsford 1st. Officer a very nice fellow indeed. We dine when all present seventeen.

If William ever takes a sea voyage let his bed be put *across* the ship and not fore and aft, as I have had not a few spills out of bed and then after tucking myself in from the roll of the ship all the clothes roll off, whereas across the ship you only have to shift your pillow according to the side the vessel heaves in order to keep your head uppermost – and let the basin be a *deep one* (this also may apply to himself) as from the shallowness of my Brass one with the least roll, over goes the water, unless I have not enough of it in the basin to wet the tip of my nose. And if he happens to have in the next cabin to himself two smoking gents as I have, he would wish as often as I do for a few pasteles, for their vile pipes are going all day long, enough to make anyone sick.

The 24th. Comet still visible at night. The island of Palma was in sight this Evening, but a long distance off. Everyone was so anxious to have a peep at any thing like solid land. Our Latitude today 29.40 North & 17.43 West.

Saturday 25th. Service performed, the Annunciation Day. Our awning put up as the sun strikes hot. Lat.27.4. & Long. 18.50.

The Bishop came to my cabin door. I was playing and therefore asked rather sharply, Who is that kicking up such a row? He said, It is the Bishop – I let him in and then told him how I was bothered when practising. He sat down and looked through my Song Book, admired the Last Man.

Sunday 26th. Our usual service on deck and a beautiful sermon from John 6, 53rd. Verse, and explaining it and giving out the Sacrament for the following Sunday. We have Service also at 7 in the Evening, but the Archdeacon preaching does not strike half so deep as the Bishop and such a wretched sing-song delivery.

Monday 27th. Nothing but fair wind and fine weather as we are in the Trade Winds.

Tuesday 28th. May. My porthole being open like the rest of the passengers in shipped a sea! I had enough to do to get out of the water, bed wet through to the sheets.

29th. I took a dose of the *good stuff* which amply performed its duty. Owing to a nail driven into a leaden pipe by one of the passengers, three or four cabins were afloat today again, so I have had enough of water.

30th. Some of the passengers looking at their Guns found them rusty, and fortunately opening my case suspecting the same – lo and behold my gun was *all* rust, at least one barrel so that I had enough to do to clean it, in fact it is two or three days work.

Lots of bugs which like one terribly. I sleep with one blanket on me, sometimes nothing at all. Light clothes are all the go and shoes of which I have *none*. (By the bye I brought no scissors, a great omission. I borrowed a pair to cut my own hair.)

31st. Lat.72.41 North. Long. 20.36 West.

1st. April, wished little Ady many additional happy years to the eleven she has just celebrated.

Sunday 2nd. April. I received the Holy Sacrament and when it was over I went to my cabin and thought of the last time I communicated in England with you all and Mr. Carlyon's valued book given me on that day (26th. Febry.) gave me much pleasure to read. Mrs. Smyth's Golden Message is a very nice little book. The Thermometer on Sunday was 78 degrees.

Monday 3rd. Wind dying off, weather hotter. I am sitting now writing with only my shirt and trowsers on. You are all I suppose carrying umbrellas to ward off the April showers. How quickly summer seems to me to have succeeded winter. A Lemonade Powder today was very grateful. Lots of flying fish and other curiosities to be seen.

Thursday 4th. We were today at 12 o'clock to the Southward of the sun, Thermometer about 82.

I shall finish your letter, my dear Mother, and seal it as I cannot put much more news into it and the rest of the news I shall put in my Father's when you see a line drawn. The news will be stale and the postage I suppose heavy, otherwise I would write to some of the others. Remember me kindly to all friends – those on the Terrace more especially and my former Pastor. Love to all relations and friends who are entitled to it. My love to all brothers and sisters and accept the same, dearest Mother, from your

very affectionate son

Henry Godfrey.

Finished today Wednesday 5th. April – just after a regular fine shower. This morning I had a delightful bathe.

All your birthdays will be remembered by me as I have them down in my book.

THE LETTER TO WILLIAM

Henry's long letter to his brother Willie is revealing in a number of aspects. He was able to write more informally to a sibling than to either of his parents and could therefore express his views more freely and in greater depth. William was the brother next to him in age, his junior by two years –

their sister Emily came between them. He evidently expected Willie to follow him to Australia in the near future and took pains to prepare him for a voyage similar to that which he was undertaking at the age of nineteen.

As things were to turn out it was to be Frederic and not William who was to join Henry in Victoria some three years later. In 1843 when the letters were written on board ship Fred was only fifteen and still a pupil at Exeter Grammar School. He does not appear to have been the recipient of an individual letter, though he is mentioned more than once in the correspondence to other members of the family. Frederic left England in 1846 and he, too, sailed in the *Duke of Roxburgh*, but the voyage must have been very different from Henry's, there being no Bishop on board and consequently very few religious services and certainly no restraint on the conduct of the passengers. He read prayers in his cabin with his cousin and her husband who were travelling out with him. Captain Collard was again in command and Mr. Lamb, who had sailed as Third Mate when Henry was aboard, had by then been promoted to the position of Second Mate.

William did eventually go to Australia, but not until 1857. He married there and died near Melbourne at the age of seventy-eight, Henry having predeceased him by twenty-four years.

Bishop Nixon must have had considerable influence upon Henry who plainly admired him greatly and held him in the highest esteem. His presence affected the general tone of the ship.

His religious faith meant a great deal to young Henry Godfrey and his attitude in this respect reflected his type of home background and his upbringing. In a class-conscious society it was to be expected he would come across people, particularly among those in his contemporary age group, who would regard him as a pious prig. However he had the strength of character to uphold his principles in the face of ridicule and although indignant at being called a Muff he could also see the funny side of it. The term used in this context implied one lacking in *savoir faire* – which was of course largely true, regardless of what Henry himself may have felt to the contrary. His life up to this time had been regular and sheltered, limited to associating principally with persons of his own sort.

One wonders how William reacted to his elder brother's homily. Did he resent such blatant sermonising as an infringement on his own moral integrity or did he accept it as well-meant advice from one experiencing the kind of problems the younger brother was likely to have to face in the future? In view of the close-knit nature of the family's relationships the latter response would seem the more likely.

In the postscript there is another reference to "dear Gussy", his second cousin Augusta Sarah (born 1820). Her brother John Bulwer Godfrey was Captain of the sailing ships *Statesman* and *Constance*. It was aboard the *Constance* that Henry was to return from Australia in the spring of 1850 and later that year she was the first passenger ship to complete the Great Circle in the record time of seventy-six days, having left Plymouth on 17 July and arriving at Port Adelaide on 1st October.

Who was this Mr. Vivian whom Henry evidently regarded as likely to be a jealous lover? We know nothing about him, though in future letters he is mentioned in disparaging terms on account of his treatment of Augusta. At this time an engagement between them is certainly implied, but they failed to marry. Three years later, in 1846, Augusta married Captain James Pearson who was twenty years older than she was. They emigrated to Australia together with Frederic and settled at Craigburn near Melbourne where their six children were born. Frederic was to make frequent references to this family in the journals he kept from 1846 onwards. When Henry returned home temporarily in 1850 he accompanied little Janet Pearson, the eldest of his cousin Gussy's children, and her nurse on board ship when she was being taken to visit her grandparents at Dartmouth. An aunt of hers brought her back the following year.

Ship. Duke of Roxburgh.
May 11th. 1843

My dear Willie,

I will endeavour to fill up this sheet to you, so as to post it when we get to the Cape, partly because, when at home I heard you complain of my not having written to you from Wales so I wish to make amends for my neglect, and partly because I wish to give you a little advice, what few brief cautions, I can with regard to you about quitting home and partly because I really have idle time on board ship whereas after I am once at my destination, I shall have little or no time to spare for superfluous correspondence, by superfluous I mean all except my dear Father and Mothers letters which I would make a point of duty, and therefore *make* time for them. Of course you will all *have* letters but not so frequently as if I were near you. The postage to my Father would become a consideration and in my leisure time I might be too fatigued after work to sit and compose – ergo *this* must last you a *long time*, it may be the end of August before you get it.

Expecting that you will at no distant period take a sea Voyage I will mention what I can about boardship routine etc. etc. Of course when I set off I made up my mind to be sick at least a week! All *stuff*. Endeavour to bear up against seasickness as much as possible – and if you are like me you will find you do not suffer so much from sea sickness for the first week as *home sickness*. However bear in mind that it was your own choice and free will to leave England and your home, you counted the cost previously – and upon that cheer yourself, and the *principal* source of comfort to you, if you *daily* pray to God and ask his guidance and blessing will be that though you are away from those you love *most on earth*, your parents: yet there is your heavenly Father who will feed you with bodily food *daily*, will deliver you from evil, and direct your steps aright, if you offer your sincere daily prayer to him as well as frequent meditations on his love and mercy towards us his children.

To continue the Routine of boardship – At 7 o'clock you rise for the first few weeks as the Mornings will be found to be cold at first. At 8 bells we have prayers read, that probably you will not have an earlier breakfast – after breakfast go down to your Cabin and if there is no Cabin boy, make your own bed, and put your Cabin to rights which I should sooner do myself than trust any boy into my Cabin. There is only myself and Mr. Lewis (a native of Van Diemans Land) who lock our Cabin doors and we have lost least of any body, he a knife, I a straw hat – but my loss is made up for the Bishop has bequeathed me his straw hat. I very much suspect the Steward's mate, a Londoner, is not overburdened with honesty. After the Cabin is tidy take a walk on the Poop or sit in the Cuddy and read, draw or play till 12 o'clock. Then a glass of sherry and a biscuit. Get the Latitude and longitude from one of the Officers; it would be advisable also, if your watch is not regulated to do so by the chronometers – so I have done. Then walk on the Poop – and read also till half past two, when dress for dinner. At six bells (3 of clock) the dinner bell rings – and pick out a place at any corner of the table, so then you will escape the pleasure of carving. The Captain sits in the middle of the table – perhaps as we sit, a description may be interesting. Every gentleman at table except Mr. P. and myself has something to carve.

	Miss Nixon	Mrs. Nixon	Captn.	Bishop	Miss Wills	Miss H. Nixon	
Archdeacon							Mr. Lewis
Doctor							Mr. Dowman 2nd. Mate
	Mr. Pritchard	Mr. Wedge	1st Officer	Mr. & Mrs. Batchelor		Mr. Godfrey	

We get over dinner by about five, sometimes later, then walk on the Poop till 4 bells (6 o'clock) tea time. After tea the sailors dance. I go out to look on – and we have managed a few times to get up a reel on the poop – but not often. If no dancing I sit in the Cuddy (as I am now) by Lamplight reading or writing. Some play chess – others walk. I prefer reading or writing after tea because the lamp is put out at 4 bells (10 o'clock) then I take my walk – and almost all turn into bed – as I use the lamplight while I can. When we approached the line the weather became very warm, I got up at half past five and walked the Poop barefoot while they wash the decks. The Archdeacon also is an early riser – and if the mornings are fine I used to take a book up to the maintop and read.

Among the amusements resorted to, is the Catching Cape Pigeons etc. etc. with fish hooks – small hooks, very thin twine, in fact thread doubled will do, but let it be blacked – you will begin to catch them about 30 South. They are the prettiest of the Southern birds I have seen – and will fly about 100 miles an hour. Mr. Batchelor shot an Albatross flying today with a bullet – also large hooks, three or four for sharks or Albatross, will afford pleasure. When you see Land at any time sketch it. Bring some good lucifer match boxes and keep them dry – mine are worthless – and the Steward offers to sell me two boxes for /6. but I tell him I will not have them, and he always laughs at me and says I shall save money – just because I will not be imposed upon! He has a number of things on board that he sells at about 200 per Cent, and from the soft ones he gets the money. I regret I did not bring an Outline Chart to track the voyage. I shall try at the Cape – and if when you leave you are asked by any kind friend or relative what you would like, say a Telescope, that is supposing you have the other requisites – Gun, pistols, Dressing Case and Writing desk. By the bye, I hope my valuable Dressing Case is made to *shine* and that none of you *young shavers* take the *shine out of it*.

My love to Fred and many happy returns to him of his birthday. Tell him to make the *most* of the time he has to spend at school, it will soon pass over his head and he never will regret having devoted his time to and profitably made use of the instruction offered to him there. He can never learn younger, he can never apply so well as in youth and if I were he, or even you, I should certainly learn the Piano so as to be able to play a little. I shall think of you all on each respective birthday.

Now I will describe some of the Characters of the Passengers, for on board you soon find out what people are and are soon upon most intimate terms or the reverse. The Bishop you must already know is a really good kind man – there is none of the clerical dignity and stiffness in him that there is in the Deans and Canons of any Cathedral Towns – but obliging in the extreme even to the sharpening a penknife – mine and many others – he has no pride. Mrs. Nixon is a very nice person, but seems rather affected, it may be her actual manner, but it is not *too* pleasing. She is more distant than the Bishop, and is not *generally* such a favourite, but she is kind enough to me, so I must not complain. The Archdeacon is a truly good mild Christian man – he has become a great favourite for his good nature and charitable disposition.

Miss Wills and myself never say a word to each other except on the subject of Dartmouth and it is such a treat to me to talk to somebody who knows the dear place so well. The Bishop is forty on the 1st August. Mr. Wedge is a nice sort of old Blade, but hard to make any way with. Mr. Pritchard is going out as a Lawyer of some sort, he is a middle aged man and has improved upon acquaintance. The Doctor I have *found out* and proved I do not like him, ditto Mr. Dowman our 2nd. Mate, and 3rd. Mate also. Mrs. Batchelor has done all my needle and thread work and is a general favourite for her retiring quiet disposition, tho' her good looks are not first rate, but much greater a favourite is she (without good looks) for her affability than Mrs. Nixon with her good looks and cold reserve. I ought not to say so much against Mrs. N., I might like her if better known. Mr. Batchelor is not yet a Revd. but will be ordained by our Bishop at the Cape or Hobart Town.

It is a great source of comfort to me to have come out with the Bishop on account of having Services and proper observance of the Sabbath as well as the Blessing of the Holy Communion the First Sunday each month. My prayer after the service is that it may please God to spare my dear Father and Mother's life and guide me through all dangers and difficulties of this world that we may see each other on earth once more. This great blessing you are not likely to enjoy because Bishops and Archdeacons are not *common* birds of passage.

And now my dear Willie for a few words of advice, and from my *short* experience of the world I think I am able to give it. There are on board some three or four persons who dislike me very much. The reason is obvious, it is because I will not take pleasure in their blasphemies and low language, but always tell them of my abhorrence of such ways and words. We are of course on friendly terms and speak to one another, but I hear what they say of me behind my back, through others. They call me a *religious Muff*! one that has seen nothing or knows nothing of the World!! Now this want of knowledge of the world consists in not joining them in their low conversation. While the Bishop is on the Poop they will be guardedly cautious of their words – directly his back is turned they abuse him in every way, calling him the worst of names; while talking to one another not a sentence is uttered without its accompanying oath – and I am a *Muff*! because I do not sit in their cabin and smoke my senses away in company with them – and I do not take pleasure in their low conversation. I tell you this because wherever you are you will meet with young men of this *stamp* who would wish to be considered *gentlemen* and I hope you will leave home with the *very firmest* of resolutions not to join the company of such, not to listen to any of their filthy talking or even worse their oaths, but show your dislike either by words or deeds. Do not be alarmed at what they can say or do. They tried very hard to laugh me out of my sense of what is right. They tried the same with Mr. Pritchard & Lewis. Mr. L. was a great friend of theirs at one time, but now he sees the folly and wickedness of their ways, and is not so familiar with them. Hear all they say of you or to you with perfect indifference except when you hear the name or service of God abused and then show your abhorrence of it and tell them plainly of the enormity of the crime. – "Fear not them which kill the body, but rather fear him which is able to destroy both body and soul in hell." – They will not do these things before the Bishop because they wish to be well thought of by him or are afraid of his rebuke, but they fear not to abuse their Creator!! and therefore I beg of you to determine not to follow their ways – not that *your* best resolutions or mine are of *any avail* without fervent prayer to God for the guidance and assistance of His Holy Spirit. We can do nothing of ourselves – yet we may say with the confidence of St. Paul "I can do *all* things *through Christ* which strengtheneth me." Now the whole of this is – Pray daily and fervently to God, to whom we can pray through our blessed Mediator and Advocate for his guiding Spirit of grace to give us power to resist and overcome all temptations and to support us under all trials and troubles of this world – and to give us *all* we pray for through Christ and *even now* knowing our necessities before we ask and our ignorance in asking. And also pray in the language of Bhp. Wilson, (all things are possible to him that believeth.) Yes Lord, and therefore I beg that *Truth* of him to whom all things are possible, that I may be able to *discover*, to *avoid*, to *resist* and to *root out* whatever evil is in me!

And now dear Willie I know you will not regret that your letter, or at least half of it, is filled up with a sort of lecture. I do it that you may be prepared for the *worst* – not that I fancy you are not steady because I doubt that not – but still there is no harm in telling you what I have met with! Although I have not told you *half* what is said to me. Yet you will know what to expect and how to act.

British Queen Hotel. Cape Town.
Tuesday 16th. May.

Here we are safely landed and as a Vessel is to sail tomorrow I will send
this off by it with a few particulars from the day I wrote last up till now, and
I have a joint letter to Louisa and Emily in hand which I will send before I
leave Cape Town with my doings here.

Sunday the 14th. The Bishop gave us a beautiful Sermon from 55 Isaiah 6
Verse. On this Evening every body fancied they saw land and therefore we
got up early Monday Morning and land was seen beautifully. I took a
sketch of its first appearance. Then after breakfast took another with the
Bishop who cuts *me out all to pieces* in the sketching line, and again I took a
third view of the Table, but the Bishop fell off the Poop and providentially
escaped a broken arm, tho' he had the breath knocked out of his body and a
sprained wrist – it is now in a sling. A Bishop in a sling is quite a novel thing
– but it might have been worse for him. However Monday at half past one
we cast anchor in Table Bay – had dinner – and the ship of course was
surrounded with boats to take Passengers off, but such an ugly set of rascals
I never saw. They looked all like pickpockets, cut-throats etc. a sort of
mongrel between Convict and Caffer, and their prices to take us on shore
were outrageous for the distance of only a mile! They asked 7/6 for the
Boat, so four of us clubbed together and beat them down to 6/-, 1/6 a piece.
We walked about the Town to look out for our abode. Boarding Houses are
all full – so we are at an Hotel. However found this a moderate one and
genteel, we did not rely on it – for I did not know whether my letters might
get mislaid. Breakfast 2/- Dinner 3/- Lunch 1/6 Tea 2/- Bed 2/- In all 10/6
separately, but staying a week the whole expences 7/6 a day – *quite enough*,
yet where are we to go? On board we cannot.

Now for my impression of the people, places etc. There are a great many
Caffers and Hottentots as well as some few Indians, known by their red
Turbans – they did not stare as much as I suspected. It is about the
beginning of Winter here and it is about as hot as Summer in England,
perhaps *not quite* so. The houses are all white-washed and low, the Streets
very regular – running at right angles to one another. We went to look at
our Church where the Confirmation is to be held – it is not unlike St.
David's in Exeter, but with a golden Cross on the top. After walking about,
with great difficulty we got a boat – the rascals wanted 12/- and then £1. At
last we found a ship's boat come for the Captain and as he would not be
ready to go on board directly we asked if they would like to earn 6/-. They
said Yes, so they pulled off with us, being dark – otherwise the Cape

boatmen would have played Old Harry with the sailors for taking us, if they had seen it. However we *did* them – and shewed them we were not in a state of *Viridity*.

We slept on board and after breakfast went off with one week's clothes in our carpet bags in the Captain's boat. I left my bag here and called on Col. Mitchell at his office – Govt. Buildings – and he had just left in his Carriage. I then went to Col. Marshall's offices and saw him – had a chat and then he took me to the Castle and introduced me to Mrs. M. who I find now to be a Miss Alexander from her asking so much about Mr. & Mrs. Jameson. She said her old Father and Mr. Jameson were great friends. She asked if he was going to be married and sundry other questions about Exeter people. She spoke very highly of Mrs. Smyth as every one that knows her do – and at last I saw the likeness in her to her *spectacled* Sisters. She said she could not offer me a bed, but I am going there to tea this evening and she has given me a general invitation to go when and as often as I like – at all hours – which is very kind, so you must not fail to thank Mrs. Smyth kindly, for me – for her letter. I wish I had known before I left England that Mrs. Marshall was a Miss Alexander. I could have taken any parcels or letters for them – and I should of course be more welcome bringing home news. I go there tonight at 7 and meet two celebrated Missionaries. When I went into their room I found a man tuning a Piano – no bad sign – well, I left them and called again at Col. Mitchell's Offices and he was not there. I find he lives some four or five miles out in the country therefore I could not take a bed of him, if he offered it, except for a night or two: I shall call again on him.

The Bishop came on shore today Tuesday 16th. The Governor's carriage and a herd of people were on the new jetty to receive him and away he drove to Government House. The Confirmation will be I believe on Thursday.

Well my dear Boy I must pray God to bless you and keep you from all evil – enjoy home while you *are* there – you will *never* be so happy again – take my word for it who have left it so lately. When you leave home and the cares of Independence come on you, you will feel yourself getting *quite old* as I do. I must finish this now as I must go and dress for the small tea party. I should not wonder if Emily's and Louisa's letters which will come the last thing, may not arrive before this one tho' sent a week before it.

And now give my love to all friends and relations near and dear – best love and kisses to dear Brothers and Sisters – each and all – dutiful and affectionate best love to my kind Father & Mother – and may God bless and prosper you *here* and fit you for the Kingdom hereafter is the prayer of your very affectionate Brother.

Henry.

I pray for each and all of you daily. I hope I am not forgotten in your prayers. Remember me more especially to the *Row* and forget not my love to dear Gussy. I must not send kisses else I should expect to see a bullet come whizzing at me all the way from England out of Mr. Vivian's pistol!

THE LETTER TO LOUISA

Louisa Madeline was Henry's eldest sister, two years his senior. Their sister Maria came between them in this family which could claim a child born on seven successive years.

The cuddy, mentioned so often as the place where services were held when the weather was unsuitable for worshippers to congregate on deck, was the Officers' cabin beneath the poop. It would seem only privileged passengers were permitted to share the convenience of this retreat at other times.

A noddy is a bird related to the terns. As it spends most of its life far from land it is unaccustomed to human beings. This would explain the remarkable degree of tameness it tends to display when it happens to come to rest on a ship. In the past this gave it the reputation of being rather stupid. Evidently Henry's father already had a specimen of this bird in his collection of stuffed skins, having obtained it from some other source.

Judged by present-day standards there would seem to have been no justification for the indiscriminate slaughter of various species of oceanic birds by shooting and also by the far crueller method of hooking them on baited lines, a pastime employed by some of the male passengers who wished to preserve the skins or simply to indulge in what they considered to be an amusing occupation. The fact that the sailors condemned this practice, believing it to bring ill luck, is of course dramatically illustrated by Coleridge in his "Rime of the Ancient Mariner".

The poop seems to have been rather an unsafe spot judging by the number of accidents sustained there in the course of the voyage. Henry implies that he himself was slightly built and thus he was not badly injured by his fall. He remained small of stature throughout his life and this physique was inherited by his third son, Ernest, who was also below average height, but his father John Race Godfrey is seen in his portraits to have been a person of considerable weight and girth.

The life of Jack Sheppard that he mentions having read was something very different from the religious subjects which seem to have been his favourite choice of reading matter. Jack Sheppard was notorious for his daring thefts and highway robberies in the early part of the eighteenth century. He accomplished four spectacular escapes from prison, each time after receiving the death sentence, but was finally executed at Tyburn in 1724, aged only twenty-two. Afterwards his activities featured in a number of popular plays, verses and romances – one of which Henry admits to have found deeply interesting.

The island of Trinidad seen in the distance on the morning of 23rd April was not, of course, the familiar island of that name in the West Indies. This one bearing the same name was many degrees further south – a small rocky outcrop off the east coast of Brazil. The trade winds must have carried the *Duke of Roxburgh* westwards right across the Atlantic before she was able to head south.

Canon Bridge (it is not spelt as in Henry's letter) stands on the River Wye not far from the county town of Hereford. The Woodhouse family lived in this area, thus it seems Colonel Godfrey was in the habit of staying with his in-laws or their near relatives so as to participate in the shooting of game birds during the month of September.

The Captain was correct in his assessment of the date when Table Bay would be reached. Frederic's birthday was 11th May so his brother's estimate of their arrival at the Cape was premature.

Ship Duke of Roxburgh,
Commenced Thursday 11th. April 1843

My dearest Louisa,

It is your turn to get a ship letter now and as the Postage of each letter is heavy (so I imagine) I will devote one half of this large sheet to you and the other to Emily, which is better than making it a joint stock sort of letter – then, each can call her half her own, which will be the *better* half I know not, but leave it to your own judgement.

Today the 11th. my Father's and Mother's letters were sealed and sent on board the "Majestic" of Liverpool from Africa. The Captn., Bishop and Archdeacon went on board her taking a sack of potatoes as a present, for which they were given the same full of "Yams" an African root like a potato. She had lots of Parrots and Monkeys on board. I think our Latitude I put outside my Mother's letter. When they returned from the ship we had Service in the Bishop's cabin and a curious circumstance, we crossed the line at 12 precisely so the latitude was 0.–0. Long. 22.16.

Thursday 13th. Heavy rain falling at intervals, everyone catching fresh water. I read through the book given by Aunt, "Confessions of an

Apostate". Service in the Cuddy – the Bishop looks very well in his episcopal robes.

Friday 14th. Good Friday – Hot Cross buns and *fasting*. Service in the Quarter Deck and a beautiful sermon by the Bishop from 1st. Tim: 15 Verse exhorting them to attend the Holy Sacrament on Easter Sunday, as usual a beautiful discourse, full of simple, intelligible instruction without any show of fine words, but straightforwardly spoken from the heart, and driven home, (so to speak.) Service again at 7 o'clock, the Archdeacon gave a Sermon "Aspice globosa terrestrium."

Saturday 15th. "Nil Scripta degressum". – Do not quiz my attempts at quoting a few Latin sentences.

Sunday 16th. We chanted the Benedictus Lit. Dominum in style, sang the Easter Hymn. The Bishop and Archdeacon both sing, Mrs. Nixon a little. I received for the second time on board, the Holy Communion. The Archdeacon's Communion Service is very handsome silver gilt. The Bishop's Service is Silver. A Noddy sat in the Cuddy during the service. I think my Father has one. The Bishop preached in the Evening from dwelling on, "Seek those things which are above," and putting the question to each of us, Have we done so? I am most thankful that by the hand of Providence which is ever leading us, and guiding our steps though imperceptibly, thankful that it was my lot to come out in this ship with the Bishop. There is by his presence such a stop put to all swearing and taking of God's name in vain – though behind his back it is the case – how much more it would have been if he were not on board to awe them by his presence. The Second Mate once made use of an oath – he did not know the Bishop was behind him – however the Bishop spoke to him about it and he was very sorry for it.

17. Monday, having taken a showerbath I had a heavy fall off the Poop, but no bones broken. The Bishop wished to have me bled, but I thought that was *no go*. I rubbed some *Trefoil Oil* of Mrs. Nixon's and took medicine. I am now writing *perfectly well*. It might have been a serious fall if I had been a heavy person. I delivered the parcel of letters for Mrs. Nixon being the day appointed by Mr. Woodcock, they were very acceptible. Service in the Cuddy.

18th. Nothing particular.

19th. Much as usual, fine weather and fair trade wind. There is a book which my Father might procure – this is the title page: "Lectures on the Catechism of the Ch. of England" by the Bishop of Tasmania – Francis Russel Nixon D.D. Late perpetual Curate of Acle next Sandwich and one of the six preachers in the Cathedral Church of Christ Canterbury – Henry Win Bridgett, Blackfriars, London 1843. An useful addition to your Library. He made the Captain accept one. I ought to have another.

20th. Today commenced the life of Jack Sheppard. Lots of Mother Carey's Chicken following the ship.

Friday 21st. All my Violincello strings broken so no more playing or singing till I get to Van Diemans Land as I do not wish to break in on my stock in the tin case which would not last long on board ship. The sea air I suppose and the dampness in the Cabin rots them. I think it would be advisable to send a Tin Case with some strings in it as soon as convenient. Have it soldered down. They are scarce articles as well as very expensive ones aboard, so Mr. Wedge asserts.

22nd. Mr. Donford our first Officer knows Col. Mitchell well to whom I have a letter from Major Osborn. A work called "Patricia" has been read aloud by the Archdeacon, but not liking his reading nor the book I pace the poop from tea time 7 till 8 o'clock when we have prayers. Aboard ship life is one of thorough idleness, one cannot sit down to any *one* pursuit for an hour at a time. My Morning from half past five till about seven is spent on the Main Top. Read from the Pious Year, Golden Treasury and Wilson. These are my Morning companions as soon as the sun rise permits reading them. I have not been higher than the Main Top Gallant Yard, nor shall I go higher, and according to my Father's advice I have not been on the Dolphin Striker on the Bowsprit. We have had lots of shooting at bottles, but I have resisted all temptation to fire my own gun tho' I've fired others.

The Bishop has a very good book of Psalms – the Title Page I send, "Manual of Psalmody" Music by B. Jacob organist of St. John's, Waterloo Bridge, printed Novello 69 Dean St. Soho. £1.1. Every body is chess playing, it is all the go. Let William have a dressing Gown. I regret the want of it in the Morning and Slippers also, 2 pr. at least – common leather better than Worsted work, or even a piece of Carpeting made into slippers would do. I do not put this because it would be interesting to you for I am aware it could not be so, but because you can extract from my letters memoranda which would be useful to William. I have perused the life of Jack Sheppard, it is a romance full of deeply interesting horrors.

Sunday 23rd. At about six in the Morning *Trinidad*, the Island in Lat. 20. 29 & Long. 29. 10 W. was in sight. We were about 48 miles from it. I took a sketch of it from the Main Yard and a more intensive view from the Main Top-sail Yard. The Bishop sketched it from the Poop, and he made it appear too close for 48 miles. This is a faint outline of it, it is rather formal. It is described as very rocky and difficult of access.

The Bishop today noticing my Prayer book's shabbiness – I have not unpacked my Father's new case – made me a present of a Prayer book which matches Aunt Ann's bible in colour. We sang the Psalms today without my Violincello as I have not yet unpacked my tin case nor do I intend to do so, but I must do so by next Sunday, or displease the Bishop and lose my important situation as Violincellist to the Bishop of Tasmania!! You ought to be quite proud of being the sister of such an important personage!! The Archdeacon gave a very good sermon this Morning and the Bishop a still better one in the Evening from 18 Numb. 46. 7–8 verses.

I suppose by this time the Oil Painting of Cannon Bridge is finished by Mr. Williams. It must of course look very pretty. I shall think of my much-to-be-envied Father on the First of September. His arrival and hearty welcome at Cannon Bridge and then the kind and polite attentions of all the young ladies there, together with the slaughter of the poor birds.

24th. A schooner came near us but did not answer our signal flag.

Tuesday 25th. Service read in the Cuddy. St. Mark the Evangelist. I'm today writing notes on each of the Bishop's sermons delivered on board. He heard I was doing so and offered to me some of his notes to copy, as his is a Skeleton sermon only a few notes & the rest spoken as the heart dictated. I shall certainly avail myself of his offer; he has also lent me his own book of Lectures or rather Sermons on the Church Catechism to read. I have begun Blunts Sermons, 3 Vols. that Maria gave me which I really *relish* now, they are truly beautiful. I read them aloud on the Poop to one of the Passengers who is generally so inclined and admires them much. Our weather is gradually getting cooler. Therm. 76 and wind rather breezy at times; to show we are approaching the Cape the Pigeons are to be seen about the ship. The Captain says the 15th. May is our landing day. I, for luck's sake, say Freddy's birthday.

26th. Nothing of note today.

Thursday 27th. Beautiful sunrises and sets to be seen, nothing like it in England. There is plenty of subject for observation to any one acquainted with astronomy. The Great Bear, Southern Cross, Milky Way, Magellan Clouds and many other heavenly bodies have been visible. Calm commenced today.

28th. The Captain offered to lower the boat if any would volunteer to pull, so four or five passengers directly volunteered, myself among them, so the Captain got us into the boat and told us to pull round the ship just to see who could pull and who not; and he turned out the Doctor and another as not being able rowers. Then the Bishop, Archdeacon and Captn. got in and Mr. Lewis and myself and a boatman pulled them about. The Bishop and Captn. took the oar at different times to relieve guard, but I kept mine all the while. In the Evening while playing Blind Mans Buff on the Poop Mr. Lewis fell off it and cut his forehead open which threw a damper on the game.

Sat 29th. At the Bishop's request the Captain again had the boat lowered and the same crew got in except for Mr. Lewis. We took Mr. Batchelor's gun and the Captain and Archdeacon shot three Mother Careys chicken. We pulled about from 12 till half past 2 o'clock. Towards evening a breeze seemed to be brewing.

The next day Sunday the 30th. was a very different sight from the calms. A stiff breeze all day and a high sea. We carried as little sail as possible and it pelted with rain. We had prayers in the Cuddy but no Communion Service or Sermon. The sailors said our rough weather was owing to the shooting of those little birds; they have a superstition about them. The change of moon was the true cause of the change of weather.

May 1st. Sunny day but stiff wind and high sea. Lots of birds – Albatross, Petrels, Cape Pigeons. Tried to hook them but *no go* yet.

May 3rd. Fine weather and *cold* enough for warm clothing again, in fact on 12 degrees each side of the line cool clothing requisited otherwise Winter clothes will do. Having *boots* I never wear stockings – shoes would have been cooler but then stockings must be worn.

Thursday May 4th. Sunny day, cool breeze and fair wind until Sunday 7th. when I again enjoyed the benefit of Holy Communion. The Bishop gave a beautiful sermon in the Evening from 6th Corinthians 19 & 20 Verses. I had my pencil and paper and took notes. I shall have nearly all his Sermons – he lent me one to copy, and seemed pleased at my doing so. I put fresh strings as he wished it and we had Psalms. A Cape Pigeon was caught for the first time.

May 8th. Every one with a hook & line catching Cape Pigeons and Petrel. The Doctor is skinning them for the Archdeacon. Albatross and every bird very plentiful. Being a fine moonlight night I played the Violincello on the Poop for the second time only. Blunts Sermons I enjoy more and more. The Bishop lent me his Sunday Sermon to make my notes on. We have a very fair wind and every body is busy writing letters to post at the Cape. I must now shut up this *half* of the shop which contains more than it seems for it is closely written. Offer my kind regards and remembrances to *all friends*. Love to all relatives near & dear, not forgetting *Gussy*. I wonder when the wedding day will arrive. My best love to my Father & Mother, sisters *each*, brothers all and accept the same from your ever affectionate brother

Henry Godfrey.

The journal will go to Emily on the other side.

LETTERS FROM CAPE TOWN

The letters Henry began to write on board ship to William, Emily and Maria were not completed until he had been able to add his impressions of Cape Town where the *Duke of Roxburgh* lay at anchor for a week in the harbour before the voyage was resumed. Emily was the sister a year younger than Henry who seems to have been known by the nickname "Meg". Alice was the youngest of the ten Godfrey children, born in 1834, four years after Adeline. Their brother's thoughts were constantly turning to the various members of his large family. He did not expect to see his little sisters again until they had grown out of all recognition. Indeed it was to be seven years before he was to return home for the first time.

It appears he had started to grow facial hair at quite an early age – or does he mean that the side-whiskers he was encouraging were not yet ready to be trimmed so Ady could not have the sample she had requested? One wonders if she ever got it. A photograph of Henry taken some time later than this period, but before he had grown the impressive beard featured in pictures of him during middle age, shows him with a small moustache and luxuriant Dundreary whiskers.

The first mention of a stye in his eye occurs in the letter dated 11th. May. This was to be a recurring trouble over the years and it will be seen he was suffering severely from inflammation of the eyes at the time of his departure from Australia in 1850.

The arrival at Cape Town was welcomed as a pleasant interlude to break the monotony of the long sea voyage. Henry was particularly lucky in that he had introductions to several people in the town who proved friendly and helpful, and also that he was to some extent a protegé of Bishop Nixon's. He found there was some resentment on the part of the local inhabitants at not having a bishop of their own to officiate at the forthcoming Confirmation ceremony, the prelate of Tasmania – an upstart junior colony – being required to performed that duty. This gave rise to the query about Nixon being a Pasquilé – the term implying they regarded him as being something of a fraud and a parvenu. Henry was quick to speak up in support of his friend. Neither was he behind-hand in giving his opinion when attending a meeting of young men, asserting that it was best to avoid controversial subjects such as politics and religion as they were the topics most likely to cause disagreement and unpleasantness when under discussion.

Although Henry gives a very vivid picture of his doings in Cape Town he says little about what he actually saw when land came in sight after three months at sea. He makes up for this by sketching the view of Table Bay

three or four times while the *Duke of Roxburgh* was at anchor there.
Ninety-four years later his two teenage great-granddaughters were also to
see the blue bulk of Table Mountain on the horizon and watch it gradually
grow nearer – in their case from the deck of an ocean liner. In common with
nineteen-year-old Henry they also reached the summit of the mountain and
looked down upon the town and its harbour three thousand feet below, but
for them and their parents in 1937 the ascent was by cable-car in a matter of
minutes, whereas the party of young Victorians tackled it the hard way. To
complete the arduous climb in three and a half hours was in itself quite an
achievement. Considering the long skirts worn by the women at that time it
was remarkable that only one girl dropped out on the way up and was
forced to wait for the others to rescue her when they descended. In this
instance Henry seems to have been the one to play the knight errant.

In his letter he mentions throwing stones at monkeys and rabbits on the
way up the mountain. Today we should regard this as a needlessly callous
pastime just as we consider the killing of the albatrosses and other sea birds
he also described as being quite indefensible. But at that time there was little
or no respect for wild life. The monkeys he saw were doubtless baboons
which are still abundant in the Cape peninsula, while the animals he termed
rabbits were assuredly hyraxes or rock rabbits, known coloquially in the
Cape as "dassies". These small furry creatures resemble rodents super-
ficially, but in reality they are distantly related to the elephant. They live in
colonies of up to fifty individuals of all ages and sizes, inhabiting rocky
terrain and making their homes in cavities beneath the boulders.

In the Cuddy of the Old Duke.
May 11th. 1843

My very dear Meg,
I shall now be able to say that you have each had a letter from me
although this is half a one it contains quite as much as I could get into a
concurrent sheet. This day last month my letters to my Father and my
Mother were sent. I suppose they have hardly got them yet. I shall continue
this as a journal. Today I drank Fred's health. We have fine weather but
rather cold, of course nothing compared with England – still compared with
our warm season just past it seems cold. How beautiful Devonshire must
look now, all the leaves coming forth. I often indulge in sweet thoughts of
home and times spent there, never to return. Our Longitude alters now.
Yesterday Lat.34.48 S. Long.1. 22 E. (the 10th.) it was. The Bishop and self
had a long walk on the Poop together, and the subject of our conversation
was chiefly Mr. Wedge and Miss W.

12th. I played Draughts in the Evening. Fine weather and fair winds.
Saturday 13th. Not being over above well I took two pills and have one
of those *pleasant* things a stye in my eye. The Capt. remarked it was a pity it
should come just as we were near the Cape. The Bishop said, Ah, Mr.
Godfrey does not care to look beautiful at the Cape today. I have been busy
getting out my clothes for the Cape. Monday morning is the expected day.

I had a great treat this Evening in looking over the Bishop's sketches in
Italy about Naples and the Rhine also. He has lived abroad some time.
They are really *Beautiful* and so beautifully touched. He has two large
Portfolios full – He pointed out all the interesting parts to me and as I
looked at them by candlelight I have begged another view of them by
daylight.

With the intense activity and interest there is caused by nearing land,
every one gazing in all quarters to try and get a peep at solid land once more
after looking upon the panoramic horizon so long. I hardly know which is
the most enjoyable sight to see a vessel bearing down upon us, we all
scribbling as hard as possible and at last to see her increasing in bulk till she
stops and then our letters sent home by her – or to behold once more the
green fields or rocky cliffs. Everyone asks – Well, Captain – how soon shall
we reach the Cape?

Tell Ady I have not harvested my whiskers yet or she should have the
sample enclosed herewith. I often think how Alice and Ady will be grown
out of knowledge if I live to see them again – I should certainly pass them in
the street. The rest of you I should more likely recognise. I myself am a deal
browner than when I left you and rope climbing and gymnastics altogether
have increased my breadth, but as for length I am yet at a standstill and
likely to win dear Papa's ring. Perhaps you did not know our agreement. If
I grow more than two inches before my return I give him a Ring – if not I
receive one.

The Bishop shewed me one of the best Photographic likenesses I have
seen, of himself and Mrs. Nixon in one picture – both with black hair and
black eyes, – by the bye, another instance of an exception to your ridiculous
rule! It is excellent. He has also another of himself alone, a bust. The two in
one are full figures, she is sitting and he standing with his arm on her
shoulder. So much for boardship.

Cape Town. "British Queen."
Wednesday Morn 17th. May.

I finished my letter to Willie yesterday Evening and sealed it so now I
continue the narrative of the perigrinations of Henry Godfrey from the

16th. Ult. When I finished his letter I put on my dress coat and Trowsers and white waistcoat I bought when I sported a white tie to set the fashions, however I did not expect to see such a lot of people. There were upwards of 25 people – lots of them young ladies. They celebrated Mr. Moffat sent out by the Missionary Society. (I believe into central parts of Africa.)

I was rather lionised having come out with the Bishop, all sorts of questions were asked me about him, Was he not a Pasquilé? and other suchlike foolish questions. I spoke up for him in fine style and I am sure I did not speak too highly of him. It seems to me that it is a sore point with these Cape people that the junior Colony, the upstart Colony of New South Wales, should have a Bishop before them. However there will be I am sure many to be confirmed as it is ten years since the last Confirmation by Bishop Wilson.

We had a little music in the evening but Mrs. Marshall was the only performer – the young ladies fingers were, I suppose, frozen! as it is the winter here, and a Mr. Stapleton played the flute, he is the private tutor of Col. Marshall. After music we had a long extemporaneous prayer by Mr. Moffat and then a supper of nice fruits, tarts, blancmange. To see the fruits was a great treat after the months on board. I find by comparison with passengers of other ships that we have had a wonderful passage not only for the shortness of time but for fine weather. I left at just past ten and being moonlight found my way from the Castle which is at the end of the Town to the new jetty which is at the other. They kindly asked me to dinner in a friendly way. I of course accepted. I had a good nights rest and am now going to breakfast.

I dined and spent the day at Col. Marshall's and in the evening went with Mr. Stapleton to a meeting of young men, they term themselves the Mental Improvement Society. They meet once a week, about 30 members, and discuss the pros and cons of any subject. When I was there it was upon different forms of Government. Mr. Stapleton was the president and took me as a visitor. I gave him my opinion that surely it would be better *not* to discuss matters in which *Politics* or *Religion* are concerned, or there are all kinds of differences here – and advocates for every different form of Government – though *Republicans* have the superiority in numbers. I said it would bring on a constant disagreeing of the members which might lead to unpleasant quarrels. He is Independent I found out by his conversation, yet he agreed with the truth of what I had remarked. I could term it the "antipeace-making Society" from the hot discussions, from the hot argument made use of by its *anti-sensible* members.

I left the British Queen this morning, 18th. May as I found it was a low house. I met the steerage passengers there and heard conversation and noisy rioting, so the three of us left it and took rooms at the George Hotel in the Heeren Gracht – there is a Dutch name for you! We put on our Sunday clothes and went to the Confirmation – to look clerical and try to get a good seat I sported a *white* tie: what with that and the Bishop's name in my Prayer book I of course got a seat, though some time they kept clerical gentlemen waiting! Standing, there were about 400 to be confirmed.

I must continue this in Maria's letter as I have no more room for you, and Believe me my dear Meg

Your affectionate Brother
Henry Godfrey.

"George Hotel" Heeren Gracht.
Cape Town.
Monday Morning 22nd. May /43

As I had not room in Emily's letter to give you all my doings at Cape Town and as my first letter sent to you after only 5 days at sea was very short, hurried & uninteresting, I feel it my duty to you, my *dearest* Maria to send you one more sheet if I can fill it all the better.

In Emily's letter I left myself *white tie* & all seeing that most imposing sight a confirmation. The Bishop gave them a beautiful exhortation from the Pulpit about the nature of the vows voluntarily taken by them and an exhortation to come to the Lords table on the Sunday following. The Church is a fine large Church with an Organ of the Capes build! it was *crowded*. A Bishop is not an every day personage in Cape Town, so Jews, Malays & dissenters of every kind were present to see & hear him. After the Service I trotted off to the Castle & came just in time for soup, after tea I left them & went by invitation to spend the Evening with Mrs. Batchelor & her husband, who are at Mrs. Huttons Boarding House Strand Street, and being dark I had a fall into a ditch but only sprained a finger or two. When I arrived at my destination a clothes brush and cold water were both brought into play & did their duty – Had a very musical Evening, there being 4 daughters who play & sing *no end*. They made me sing "Wanted a Governess" & "The White Squall" as they had there both – for I did not bring my song book on shore.

Friday Morning 19th. May. The Captain hired a Phaeton & drove Mr. & Mrs. B., Mr. Pritchard & 2 young ladies, myself & Mr. Lewis as equerries in waiting to the Constancias – for there is Great Constancia, High Constancia

& Little Constancia and we tasted the 4 kinds of wine at each different place. It was deliciously sweet. I send you a card of High Constancia & my opinion of the wines – It may be amusing. These Constancias are each a perfect Paradise with their Orange Groves loaded with fruit, their myrtle hedge walks, their Geranium & Rose hedges – every kind of delightful flower & fruit added to a charming situation & view of the sea, quite an Eden upon Earth! They are about 12 miles out of Cape Town. You can imagine how I enjoyed the day – what with the sweet *wines*, & the total novelty of the scene. I picked a number of oranges & limes to take on board. Having written all our names & the name of the Vessel, its destination etc. in the visitors Book, we set off on a beautiful road with fir & oak trees on all sides of us and the day having been very favourable we enjoyed it much although we are here in the wrong month for the grape. January & February is the best month to arrive here for fruits etc. – but May for passengers from England as they would be roasted in the other months unless they came on shore with thin clothing. I am dressed now as at home. I could not call at the Marshalls today as we have been out all day & came home tired & glad to get to bed.

Next morning 20th. at about 8 a note came from Mr. Batchelor to ask us to accompany them up Table Mountain as it appeared a fine Morning. Breakfast over, 11 of us in number began our route, with a Cooly to carry our grub & as a guide also. We began ascending at about ½ past 10 – and after fatigue, hunger, thirst, at times saying we could get no further, resting, scrambling up again, slipping and falling, after all these sensations we arrived at the top at about half past one, having left one young lady behind us on the hill, for she could get no higher. We amused ourselves throwing stones at the Monkeys & rabbits as we went up. When at the top we were amply repaid for our toil. The view is the most extensive & beautiful that imagination can picture. The ships in Table Bay looked like boats – we had a fine view of all Cape Town. We sat down with wet feet of course, for we constantly had to go through water on our way up & we were literally enveloped with clouds frequently. We sat down tired & hungry, ate our sandwiches & drank our Beer etc. when the sister of this young Lady that could get no further began to get into a *stew* about the welfare of her younger sister – and of course her starvation – for we were all raving hungry. *I*, ever the ladies man, offered to go down with some victuals for her in advance of the rest, not knowing the difficulty of the undertaking on account of finding the right *Kloof* (cleft in the rock). However off I set & after walking this way & that into each crevice I could not find the right one, so got the Malay to put me into the proper place, and then down I went. Found the poor girl in lonely solitude. I gave her the provisions & we sat down on the rocks until the rest of the party should think fit to make their appearance. We got home tired as possible & went to bed.

We went to St. Georges Service, commenced at 11 o'clock – a Mr. Blair was ordained, a very impressive Service it is. The Archdeacon gave them a very good Sermon. The Bishop said it was the best Sermon he had ever preached – he was much pleased at it – & I was highly delighted. It was chiefly on our bishops and dating their authority in every way from the Apostles in regular sucession – they from Christ & Christ sent by God. There were people of all ways of thinking in Church. I hope he benefitted them. The Sacrament was administered to all who were confirmed on the previous day & the *new priest*. I did not stay as I had not prepared myself. After Service I went to Col. Marshall's, but dining at half past one their dinner was over & I stoutly refused having it brought in again, so a glass of wine & biscuit sufficed. I took tea there. I bid them Adieu – thanking them for their kindness and they expressed a desire that I should write to them some months hence as they should always feel an interest in my welfare. I said I would write. They have been really very hospitable & friendly. Their 6 boys & one girl are all well & very plump. Cape air seems to agree with them. Mrs. Marshall is also in good health. I called this Morning & left my T.T.L. and at Government Buildings. Col. Mitchell lives 4 miles out in the country at Rondebosch so I only saw him once at his offices. He spoke very kindly & was sorry I was going on to Van D. Land. He offered to render me any assistance in his power in case I came back here to settle (Likely!).

I have just returned from Col. Marshalls having dined there (22nd. May) I am glad that I am staying at the same house as Captain Collard so I know for certain when he will leave for the ship & he has offered to take me in the boat with him – very convenient. This Evening the Captain & myself go to a Dance & expect to find a Musical Evening where there are many pretty young ladies. I send this with the Captain's letters to his Agent who will forward it by the first ship. Altogether I have spent a very pleasant week here. The Marshalls have been very kind. I shall now conclude this, dear Maria, with dutiful love to my Father & Mother, best love & kisses to all Brothers & Sisters & Gussy – also kindest remembrances to all friends, the Row especially, and accept the love of your

ever affectionate Brother

Henry Godfrey.

FINAL LETTER ON THE VOYAGE

The last of the surviving letters written during the voyage was addressed to Henry's mother after leaving the Cape towards the end of May. It includes mention of his own birthday on 4th. June when he became nineteen years old. Naturally at this time his thoughts were centred on both the past and the future. Birthdays figured significantly in his reminiscences and he never forgot to think of the members of his family on the appropriate dates. Several others occurred in the course of the voyage, including that of Archdeacon Marriott who was then only thirty-two. Bishop Nixon, too, was a relatively young man to hold his exalted position; he was forty at this time.

There is no indication as to the nature of the illness threatening to prove fatal for thirteen-year-old Fanny Nixon, the eldest of the Bishop's three little girls. Did she die on board ship, as Henry feared was all too probable, or was she destined to linger on until Tasmania was reached on 19th. July? We have no means of knowing. The severity of her illness obviously had a depressing effect upon all those on board.

Nevertheless, the letter ends on a somewhat lighter note. Henry, with the critical intolerance of youth, was both amused and affronted by observing a romance developing between the two unattached middle-aged people he had got to know in the course of the voyage. Mr Wedge, the much-travelled pioneer, was attracted to Miss Wills, the Nixon children's governess. One wonders if his admitted confusion in addressing them by the wrong names was not, in part at any rate, deliberately provocative. As it happened, he had no reason to have been scornful of a love affair between persons whom he considered to be old. We shall see the sequel to this shipboard romance is mentioned at a later date.

No further letters exist dating from this period. This one to his mother was the last to have been copied out by his father and it is incomplete, ending in the middle of a sentence without even a full stop, as if John Race Godfrey was interrupted in transcribing from the original and never resumed the task he had carried out so assiduously up till then. Thus there is no record of Henry's arrival at Hobart or subsequently at Port Phillip, though we do know he did not set foot on the mainland of Australia until 15th. October 1843, one hundred and twenty-six days after leaving home.

Duke of Roxburgh.
24 May 1843

I again resume my pen on board to proceed with my journal for the regularity of which I hope, my dearest Mother, you will give me all due credit. Yesterday Morning the 23rd. we left the Cape after having spent a very pleasant week there, the weather for the time of year having been particularly favourable for sightseeing, sketching etc. Away we went with a favourable wind, the land looking small by degrees & beautifully less, till the mountains were concealed by the distant horizon. We all felt rather qualmish after a weeks run on terra firma. The ladies, the Bishop & a few of the gentlemen were sick, but I managed to escape it, although not without frequent *peculiar* internal sensations next akin to sea-sickness. Today the Queen's Birthday was not forgotten by her most loyal subjects on board the "Duke" and we drank "the Queen" with all our hearts. We saw in the distance 2 homeward ships with the sun shining on their white sails, an object of great interest at sea – every body *must* have a look through the Telescope at them. The Thermometer is 62, our Lat. 34. 30 So. Long. 17.46 East. I went to bed, having at my own discretion bolted 2 pills.

May 25th. was a fine day but the wind foul & the Service for Ascension day performed in the Cuddy. I pricked out my track from England to the Cape on a Chart procured there & marked it in red ink. An awning was erected on the Poop & the ladies & children had an awning much to their gratification & our amusement. Chess playing as usual in the Evening, there are 2 sets of men.

26th. A fine day & very little wind – & for the first time we saw Albatrosses caught with a large hook & line & a bit of the skin of the Pork attached – 4 were caught directly after each other, and all four were differently marked and coloured. The largest measured 9 feet 10 ins. from wing to wing. They were instanteously killed by pouring 3 or 4 drops of Prussic acid down their throats. One of them was *let go*. The other 3 skinned by the Sailors, one for the Archdeacon, one for Mr. Wedge & the 2nd. Mate had the 3rd.

27th. The Archdeacon today attained his 32nd. year and of course his health proposed and drunk. A fine day, but the wind still unfavourable.

28th. Was a beautiful day. The Service on deck, the *vice organ* did its duty & the Bishop gave us a good discourse. The Archdeacon having singularly selected the same test as the Bishop's for his Evening discourse, was obliged to preach another – which he did extempore, exhorting all to come to the Holy Sacrament on the following Sunday.

29th. A thick fog all the Morning till dinner time & then the wind became fair. With the money collected by the Sacrament, there being no sick on board, the men were given a shirt & cap apiece and the ladies are all busy marking them with the words [there follows a blank space in the writing so there is no telling what motif was worked on the shirts – unless, of course, it was the name of the ship, which would seem the obvious choice] in red worsted; my device having met with the Captain's approbation he appointed me as the marker, so I marked the letters on each shirt with white chalk & the ladies worked them with red letters on the deep blue shirt very nobly.

30th. was a fine day, the wind fair – but nevertheless I managed to catch a cold of some body. I think Mrs. Batchelor brought it from the Cape. The Bishop's hand is still very painful from the effects of the sprain he had on the 15th, which I think I mentioned.

31st. Birthdays seem often to happen on board, today Fanny Nixon lays claim to the attainment of her 13th year – poor creature she is much worse & looks miserably ill. It is the last birthday she will spend on Earth in all probability! But God's will be done.

1st June was quite an English June day, wind favourable. My cold is on the mend. Fanny Nixon much worse & they seem low about her.

2nd. A Squall got up & at 4 in the morning I got up to see it. Lightning frequent & bright. Morning dark, wind howling, sea rising, ship rolling, rain falling – what a contrast & how sudden a change from the day previous! The rain & wind continued all day and we could hardly be clad warm enough. Therm. 57.

3rd. The same day as yesterday & tremendous sea running, rolling all night. Things in the Cabins tumbling about in prime style.

4th. Fine! My first birthday spent at sea! Many thoughts occupied my mind & I was inclined to be "il penseroso" all day. Many new resolutions came with my new year which I pray for divine assistance to be able to keep & act up to. One great disappointment to me was that we could have neither Service nor the Sacrament of which I had wished to be a partaker & which would have been a very good beginning, an act suitable to a *Birthday* more particularly in as much as one would wish by God's grace to date from that day our "death unto Sin", and "our new *birth* unto righteousness" sealing & certifying our resolutions to lead a better life, asking for the help of Gods Holy Spirit to be able to do so (from whom the very will to live cometh) and praying for forgiveness of sins past through Jesus Christ in that Sacrament. We all read to ourselves and walked as well as we could for it was blowing heavily & a high sea running. I had the gratification of tasting some cake made at the shop leading into the Cathedral Yard – Broad Gate or East

Gate, I forget which – that the Archdeacon procured then and reserved for my birthday. The Steward also made me a large Cake which came on table after dinner & lasted till the Wednesday following. At 7 in the Evening being rather still we had the prayers only. The Sailors also in the Morning were disappointed of sporting their newly received and marked shirts on Whit Sunday. At about 12 at night Mrs. Baily added one to the list of our Passengers, making up to now 70 Souls. She is the wife of the Bishop's Servant, so my birthday was honoured.

5th. A slight gale in the Morning with showers which increased and mounted in value to a *gale* of wind. We were running fortunately before it with only a presail and close reefed topsails, the waves reaching upon the Poop and the ship rolling awfully – actually a grand sight.

6th. A moderate edition of yesterday's weather. A Sea pie for dinner which consisted of two ducks, two fowls and a leg of mutton, potatoes, onions and carrots all stewed in a large boiler or saucepan which said boiler is brought into the Cuddy and the Steward bales out a plateful each. It is only resorted to in the roughest weather when no dishes would stand on the table. As a novelty most of us enjoyed it. We really have lived like fighting cocks (so to speak) an excellent table kept all the Voyage. The Captain brought some excellent wine at the Cape; the Bishop has relieved him of one Cask of it, 19 Galls:, but after all no wine for me like Constancia, not for a constancy but for a Sunday and birthday wine, the prices of it I sent home on a Card. I should have sent a Cape Paper but forgot it, in the *press of business*!

7th. Wind rather abated but cold and the ship steady enough to permit me to *grumble* on the *growler* as it has been erected for some time.

8th. The Captain having expressed an intention of having an arm chair made, for his seat at the Cuddy table was by no means agreeable when carving – all the draughtsmen sent their demonstrated ideas upon the subject, the Bishop and all, and my plan was honoured with his approbation, and the Chair – "The *new* Arm Chair" in distinction to Aunt Ann's old one, is in the course of erection.

> "I love it, I love it, and who shall dare
> To question my right to this new Arm Chair?"

9th. Cloudy day but no rain. A large whale was to be seen going round the ship, spouting at intervals, and exposing to view his huge carcase.

10th. A foggy morning, but it cleared up by midday. Last night the Doctor sat up with Fanny. A few days it is likely she will linger on or may be more. I hope she may be landed in Hobart-Town, for I can fancy nothing more awfully impressive than a death on board and the commital of the body to the deep! I have made another attempt at composing a Chant. It will be prime rubbish when I come to hear it performed on the Piano.

Chess-playing is the rage every Evening, the Bishop is very partial to it, and is a good player, but the Archdeacon is a better player. I am now writing, 7 o'clock (about 2 o'clock with you) with two sets of Chess played about me – the Bishop & Mrs. Nixon, the Captain & Mrs. Batchelor. Miss Wills is opposite *seems* to be making Baby linen! whether for Mrs. N. or herself! I cannot tell. But I really think it will be a case of Splice; I mentioned in a former letter Mr. Wedge's unreserved attention – the *ramble* together at the Cape did wonders I imagine. It is *ludicrous* to see an ugly old man of 50 in love – to watch his motions; young men look foolish *enough*, but old men much worse. I constantly am guilty of sad mistakes, calling her Miss Wedge and him Mr. Wills. I made such *lapsus linguae* as that this evening. I saw them cast a "coup d'oeul" at one another.

It is a fine moonlight night so I shall not sit in writing, but go and have a turn on deck. Being Saturday Night the Sailors are fiddling and dancing: their usual night of rejoicing. The weather now for winter is uncommonly fine.

11th. Today the weather contradicts my last assertion. We were not able to have the Sacrament on Whit Sunday and now Trinity Sunday has brought with it the same weather. We had prayers said by the Bishop and *desired* for Frances Maria Nixon! In the evening the same. I could not enjoy a moonlight walk this evening for it is pouring and at intervals flashes of lightning. So my Cabin is my refuge.

12th. Is a blowing day.

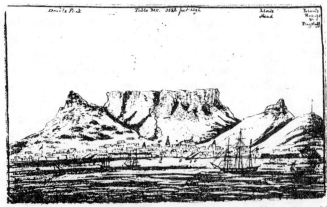

Sketch of Cape Town and Table Mountain by Henry Godfrey. June 22nd. 1843

4

Down Under

There is no record of Henry's arrival in Tasmania apart from the fact that the ship berthed at Hobart on 14th. July 1843. During the next few months he must have assessed the situation with regard to settling in the island, but decided to move over to the mainland – probably following advice given him by Mr. Wedge, that seasoned old campaigner who knew that the chances for a young man with only limited means of making a living off the land were better in the undeveloped Australian outback than in the relatively small areas available in Tasmania. There, a considerable proportion was already stocked or under cultivation, and there was a certain amount of hostile competition between the rehabilitated convicts and the independent colonists who had arrived later.

Consequently Henry reached Melbourne on 14th. October. At all times he refers to the colony as a whole as Port Phillip – the name now confined only to the bay and its immediate environs where the city of Melbourne stands. The area was so named in order to commemorate Captain Arthur Phillips, the first Governor in Australia, who came to Botany Bay in command of a fleet of ships bringing convicts to the newly established penal settlement in 1788. It was not until 1850 that this south-eastern corner of the continent became known as the State of Victoria in honour of the Queen.

We next hear of Henry Godfrey early in 1844 when he was staying with Mr. Bear and his wife at their cottage near Melbourne. Presumably he had been given an introduction to Mr. Thomas Bear by a mutual friend. Bear was a man who had already established more than one sheep station in the region and he was to prove a staunch ally and adviser to the youngster from England during the succeeding years.

The first letter we have belonging to this period is a single sheet closely written on both sides and headed with an asterisk which seems to indicate it was the final portion of a longer letter, the rest of which has been lost. For this reason it bears no date, but in it Henry remarks he has recently written to General Boles. In later correspondence there is reference to the letter to the General having been written on 24th. February 1844, thus this fragment

53

to his mother must date soon after that. In it he comments on the disgraceful treatment his cousin Augusta has received. Evidently she had been jilted by the Mr. Vivian to whom she was engaged to be married. He makes repeated references to this matter in the other letters he wrote home during 1844. It was something that troubled him greatly.

By this time, some six months after arriving in Australia, the young man was established in his own station at Gobur which is situated close to a creek running into the Goulburn River. (He spells it Goulbourn – and sometimes adds an 'e' at the end.) It is about eighty miles north-east of Melbourne, due east of the present-day town of Seymour and west of Alexandra. He seems to have obtained the land thanks to the influence of the redoubtable Mr. Bear.

He soundly condemns the conduct of a fellow settler whose sharp practices shocked and disgusted him – all the more so because the person concerned happened to be the son of a bishop! It is interesting to note he had kept in touch with the highly esteemed bishop of his acquaintance, Charles Nixon, whose friendship and example he had valued so greatly on board ship and whom he was to mention several more times in future letters.

In this first letter and again in a later one, he refers to "this melting down" being a splendid system. This meant the boiling of sheep carcases in huge cauldrons so as to produce tallow from the animal fat thus obtained. In the days before refrigeration, the only way of preserving meat was by salting and, as there was insufficient demand for large quantities of salted mutton, a great deal of wastage resulted after the beasts had been slaughtered for their fleeces. This boiling-down process proved an economical method of utilising the surplus carcases and the resulting tallow provided the basis for candles – the only means of lighting in the outlying districts.

When Henry left Tasmania it seems that Mr. Wedge had given him a bloodhound puppy, but on going ashore at Melbourne on 14th. October he evidently lost it straight away. That he should have found the dog again almost six months later was surely a most extraordinary coincidence – one wonders who had cared for it all that time and how he could have been so sure the dog was his.

He writes optimistically about the likelihood of his future prosperity in the colony and envisages a garden stocked with fruit trees and vegetables when the requisite stones and seeds have been sent out from England; however, in making this request, he forgets to allow for the seasonal variations between the two hemispheres.

At the end of this letter he remarks that he has to finish it "as paper tells me to" implying there was no room to write any more on the single sheet he used. He did, however, make good use of all available space by often crossing over the horizontal lines with more script, though this made both extremely difficult to read.

FIRST LETTER FROM AUSTRALIA. EARLY 1844

If I were myself well supplied I could not in justice turn a man away for no fault whatsoever, therefore he must not depend on my employment, wages are from £15 to £20 a year for shepherds, and rations (but I think they will be lower yet, for emigrants have come & more are expected.) I am sorry to hear of Dr. Mill's eyesight; of General Boles' illness. I have written him a long letter, perhaps you will be kindly allowed to see it, because my letters to friends being written more slowly & painstakingly – I dare say I take more pains to mention things which in the freedom of a letter for home I do not particularize. To Gus also I have written for she sent me such a kind letter – poor girl. She has been disgracefully treated; but it is my firm belief it is in the end for the best; and feel personally she will eventually, if not already, trace the hand of Providence extended for her welfare and good – "His ways are not our ways, nor his thoughts ours." I said little to her on the sad subject, as the letter coming of consequence so long after the event might recall unpleasant feelings and open a healed wound.

One of my sisters says "Poor Mr. Cummings, the blacks have destroyed his crops and his Banker failed etc." She must have dreamt it, penned & posted in a trance! but pray let not Mr. Holroyd be made aware of his proceedings through me! Young Philpotts is on the Devil's river not far from me. Some say he is steady & others not, – I hear he was guilty of a shabby trick with his wool this year. He makes it worse boasting of his cleverness – namely putting all the good & clean fleeces of wool outermost in the Bale & filling the centre with bad wool. It is such proceedings as this that bring down a storm of abuse on the settlers of Port Phillip generally through the roguery of a crafty individual. Mr Octavius Philpotts – this is not well for a Bishop's son!

Towards the close of my Father's letter he writes (I have been particular in answering his queries or doubts) "I trust I may live long enough to hear that you are firmly settled & do not regret your present position; but should it be otherwise be candid & let me know as it will not be too late for you to go to India" &c.

If my dear Father by providence you are spared to read this letter of mine, you have lived long enough to hear that I am firmly and comfortably settled, and praised be to God for his mercies – I do not in the least regret my choice of life or present position – nay more, I would not change it now for any other employment or occupation in any other country or climate. I am perfectly happy and thank God quite well & contented. As for my fortune – "Cast thy burden on the Lord & he will maintain thee" the Bible tells us. Also "For bodily exercise profitieth little, but Godliness is profitable unto all things" having the promise of the life that is now and of that which is to come. So may the God of grace grant me that holiness without which no man shall see the Lord and stablish, strengthen me in every good work that my soul may be saved!

I have just written to the Bishop apologising for the liberty taken in directing so many of my letters to his care – also thanking Mrs. Nixon for her lines to my Father. I have mentioned to the Bishop the memorial window in St. Saviour. Mr. Breton also will shortly receive a letter from me. I am going to Melbourne & will post these letters, but when up again shall not probably go to town till November or Wool time & in the interim hope to write a letter to each & all of my correspondents – taking down almost a dray load of them! The Bush is a place to write letters, your thoughts are brought to bear wholly on the one subject, you are uninterrupted & therefore you will find the difference in this letter & my other ones – which being written in town and where always is a bustle – they must have been unconnected & full of faults, tautology & bad grammar, but I hope all these have been excused. If I sat down to write a formal letter as I would to the Bishop, first making a fair copy – writing home would prove an annoyance to me, and I am sure the letters would not be half as acceptable to you – whereas writing home as I do without fear of criticisms being passed on my composition or grammar, it is a pleasure to sit down & converse as it were with you, my ideas flowing as fast as my pen chooses to write them.

We were 133 from the weighing to casting anchor and 125 days actual sailing so you have fairly won the bets. A settler hearing I was writing for the above-mentioned things from home, begged me to write for him 2 pair plush trowsers and one pair high boots, saying he would pay me. I am writing to fulfil my promise, but do as you like about sending them. My brother Willie's arrival will not be hailed with less joy on my part should he be accompanied by a little Port & currant wine, some jams and a cheese, and a few pickles. If you have a few seeds of those Portugal onions that ran to seed when I was at home, I should much like them sent with the saddle &c. They would thrive here – also lots of peach, apricots and greengage, Nectarine *Magnum Bonum* stones out of Pennsylvania No. 5. How foolish of me – it will not be the fruit season when this arrives (at least I hope not) at all events if not procurable this time, send by the next opportunity.

On the 17th. I found in Melbourne the Bloodhound Puppy given me by Mr. Wedge and lost on the 14th. October/43, so it will go up to my station shortly. I left Gobur on 14th. February & got into Melbourne on 16th. My Mare I find broken, but wretchedly poor – the breaker however says I must keep her forthwith or I shall never master her. The Mare and foal will have cost me £26.8., it is a high price, but *everything* is looking better. All stock has risen in price and I think affairs are righting themselves & will now be on a firm footing. A neighbour of mine sold 200 Ewes (of the same kind as mine) at 6/6 a head with nothing given in. I bought at 6/- and my own alone is worth £100. There is great demand for them. This melting down is a splendid system and will be the cause of healing the unsound state of the Colony. I saw Wrey, to speak to, for the first time on Feb. 17th. He is looking the complete ghost of misery and ill health – he had just received a letter from home per "Wallace" now come in with Emigrants, and says he expects to have the first Government appointment that is vacant through Sir T. Acland's interest. Poor fellow – he is always planning or expecting some great boon. He will wait long enough here before an appointment will be bestowed. Young Bear was to have had the first – and where is it?

I must be closing this, my dearest Mother, as paper tells me to do so. Mr. Bear knowing how I am situated about money insists on my not stopping at the Prince of Wales – so I am writing this at his cottage. As soon as I came here I should have been done or "picked up" as the expression is, had it not been for Mr. B. A young man could not bring a better letter than to him – he knows every Settler's circumstances etc.

Give my affectionate & dutiful love to my Father. May it please God to spare him to us all for many years to come is my earnest prayer. Love & kisses to each & all my dear brothers & sisters at home & dear John abroad. My kind remembrances to all Exeter or Devonshire friends – more especially my Pastor & friend Mr. Carlyon, and accept dearest Mother, the heartfelt affectionate love of your grateful & dutiful son

Henry Godfrey – Settler!

I have not seen Mr. Cumming since 19th. Dec. and he does not yet know I am settled. Remember me kindly & especially to Mr. & Mrs. Holroyd.

The next letter was dated 25th. April 1844 and was addressed to his father. In it he showed a commendable concern for the animals in his care. Sheep and horses were continually getting lost in the bush and much time was spent in searching for them, often in very difficult conditions. He realised that the erection of fencing to enclose a large paddock would be a worthwhile undertaking as it would prevent the animals from straying.

When he had found his lost mare after spending two and a half days looking for her, Henry wasted no time riding the twenty-six miles to Goulburn, venue of the seasonal races. He was too late to watch the horse-racing and neither the bevies of lovely ladies present nor the abundance of strong drink available attracted him, but simply the prospect of a good dinner. For the majority of settlers it was the drink which took precedence over the ladies and Henry was castigated for being so abstemious in this respect. Nevertheless he won general acclaim by singing appropriate songs of a humorous vein and the evening ended with him being declared a definite asset to the community. His ability to sing was to prove an asset on many occasions during his life.

The behaviour of his neighbour who abandoned two horses, leaving them tied to trees while he sought shelter at Gobur during a wet night and was then unable to find them, aroused Henry's understandable indignation. Further instances of his disapproval of this man Fry were to occur later on.

At this stage he did not own a dog capable of hunting kangaroos or of driving away the native dingoes that worried the sheep. After helping a neighbour whose dog had killed a large kangaroo, Henry found the meat was delicious when cooked in various ways and it also provided good food for his sheep dogs. The rough life he was leading agreed with him and his parents must have been happy to hear how well contented he was in the remote locality where he had chosen to live.

It was not surprising that visitors to the station should have taken the twenty-year-old lad to be the owner's son rather than the owner himself. There must have been much laughter in the family at home when this passage of the letter was read out – though it is a letter exceedingly hard to decipher because each side of the folded sheet is written cross-wise over the horizontal lines penned in a neat flowing hand.

Gobur. Goulbourne.
Port Phillip.
April 25th /44

My very dear Father,

I must account for these few worthless enclosed lines to you. The Settler that took Ady's letter only went half way to Town when he was prevailed upon by some Bush Ladies to stay till the Goulbourne Races were over – so he returned here, and rather than allow him to go this time without the latest from Gobur I devote a few lines to you to write up my diary and add all's well.

14th. April. Sunday was a thoroughly wet day so I sat in my hut all day long before a blazing fire reading Baxter's Saints' Rest.

15th. Showery all day. A settler who has brought Philpott's run stopped the night.

16th. One flock of my sheep had been rushed, so off I rode to find them and succeeded after a short gallop through the most probable places in the Bush. I found two very large ants' nests, which I took at first to be the graves of some Blacks, but upon digging down they presented a honeycombed appearance and were full of ants. They were where the Blacks place their dead – in a tree.

Two more settlers going to the Races had a shake down at Gobur – Graves and Phillips. The latter is a son of some medico in the Queen's household.

17th. Wet all day. Nothing done but the slaughter of two fowls for dinner.

18th., 19th. & part of 20th. were spent in looking for my mare. She had hid herself somewhere in the Bush, so I was late to see the Goulbourne Races which took place on 19th. & 20th. about 26 miles from my station. I was much vexed to be the *only* Goulbourne settler away – and I resolved the first money I get whether wool money next season or your remittance – to get up a horse paddock of 100 acres fenced in, then I shall not lose days hunting the Bush through for a stray horse. I was not however to be done out of a good dinner, so having found her on the 20th. at 2 o'clock p.m. I set off & rode the 26 miles to the race dinner. The ladies of the district mustered very strong on the course, I hear, but the chief attraction to the settlers was the *Grog* to which they made themselves slaves in the evening – for I could only find two perfectly sober besides myself. They called me teetotaller and everything else. I gave them my opinion in singing the song so called, laying stress on the verse –

Since good liquor doubtless was sent for our uses
To gladden our hearts while we *shun* its abuses.

The song however made all things right with them, and it was unanimously carried that I was a great acquisition to the settlers of the Goulbourne in the vocal way, so I did not give offence by my abstemiousness – which was my desire.

On the Sunday 21st. I left, but with great difficulty – they all intended keeping it up for two or three days, and wanted me to stay – but I should have ill-spent God's holy day, so I gladly left the noisy scene & got safe to Gobur where I performed my usual Sabbath evening's duty.

22nd. & 23rd. nothing of interest.

24th. Mr. Fry, who is with me, on his way from my neighbour Websters lost himself in the Black Range and tied his horse & a mare he was leading to a tree of a dark rainy night and came down to Gobur at about 12 p.m. shivering with cold, as you may imagine – (though you know not the difficulty of finding one's way in the Bush.) He has not heard or seen anything of them since, so in all probability the horse is starved and the mare gone elsewhere with the saddle & bridle. He will never hear the last of leaving his horses to starve. His plan was to have slept in the Bush by them. For *that one* night's indoor rest he has had many days of anxious search and toil besides loss. I have been up the range for him. I have shepherded my flocks while my men went up, but in vain.

27th. Shot a dog because he would not go after a wild dog close to the sheep fold. Such is the fate of useless & cowardly dogs here.

29th. Busy drafting Ewes all day. In the evening I set off over the Black Range with a settler whose dog had killed a Kangaroo about six miles away. It was as big and tall as myself, but being the first I had seen it seemed very huge. After great trouble (for the two of us could scarcely lift it) we got it on my "Fairy" and walked home with it by moonlight, losing our course twice in these thickly-timbered ranges and down a very steep descent. It was however worth the trouble, for I have the skin and next day we had Kangaroo steaks and Tail soup – both first rate dishes – and the carcase was good feed for my dogs.

1st. May. Fine weather still – mornings foggy & cold. The fog does not disperse now till about 9 a.m. I shot a wild duck and drake in the hole opposite my hut. They are getting very numerous in the creeks now. I have also shot one or two Eagle Hawks – the other day 3 crows at a shot. One had a white eye and a red eye – the other two had brown eyes. Many crows have two white eyes – but this was a variety.

2nd. My ewe and lamb flock at the out station rushed by two native dogs. Oh that I had a good swift Greyhound or Kangaroo dog!

I hope the instructions given about my saddle will be attended to by the purchaser, whoever he is, – I am looking forward with pleasure to the receipt of the Boxes. I hope, please God, to send you home my Station accounts after a twelvemonth's trial and though I shall be the loser for the first year or two I have the satisfaction of knowing that I have not yet spent one improper or unnecessary shilling and I can conscientiously write so, because it is the truth. I taste not liquor when in Melbourne, except dining out where etiquette requires it, and though I say it that should not say it – I am steady as a Clerk – but as Mr. Powell's song words it – "I know I'm a moral young man, but am sadly afraid it won't last."

But I feel glad at being able to write that the climate agrees with me, as I have passed a summer here, that I enjoy the roughness of my life and sometimes feel I would not envy Prince Albert when riding on my run with my dog after me, where I can go as I like and do as I choose, for I am monarch of all I survey! But I hope my joy and comfort will never cause me to forget the great Giver of all Good, who has blessed and protected me from Childhood until now.

May 3rd. While talking to my shepherd at the out station two people came up and asked him whose Station they were approaching? "Mr. Godfrey's" said the shepherd. They looked me in the face and said "Are you Mr. Godfrey's son, Sir?" "No." I said, "I am Mr. Godfrey." It amused me much.

There are very many smashed settlers going home now, what a pretty account they will give of the country! They, however, have only themselves to blame.

Now a few *Colonialisms* will amuse you and help to fill this paper.
"No flies about him" means he is a good sort of fellow, or it applies to a horse.
"Rattling tack this" would be applied to a nice dish of anything.
"Merrijig you" – you are a capital fellow.
"Plenty gammon about him" needs no explanation.
"He is a Sujee sort of chap" a mean, poor couraged fellow.

But I cannot think of half of them because I wish to do so – so must close this by desiring my kind remembrances to the Holroyds, Boles, Mills, the *musical* Row and all friends. My love to all relatives – more especially those nearest of kin, Sisters, Brothers & my dearest Mother, and accept the dutiful & affectionate love of an ever grateful son

Henry Godfrey.

Next comes a very long letter written to his mother and begun on her birthday, 14th July 1844. In that year she reached the age of forty-seven.

In Australia it was then mid-winter – a season of heavy rain and rather surprisingly not a few sharp frosts. Henry complains of being constantly wet owing to the lack of waterproof clothing.

He makes no bones about his dislike of the majority of the Colonists whom he has come across. His opinion of Mr. Fry culminated in a show-down when the young man told the other exactly what he thought of him. Soon afterwards Fry left the district for good – to Henry's considerable relief.

Although leading a solitary existence he was fortunate in having plenty of resources and occupations to fill his time, which helped to prevent him feeling lonely. He made good use of his tool chest – an acceptable gift thoughtfully provided when he had set sail in the spring of 1843 by his uncle, Francis Woodhouse, the youngest of his mother's brothers.

The washing-time mentioned more than once was an obligatory practice before shearing. The sheep were driven through a fenced-off channel in the river in order to cleanse their fleeces of the dust and grime sticking to the wool, in much the same way as they are now forced to pass through a trough of disinfectant so as to kill parasites. The workers Henry employed to do this job were fortified with tots of rum, which explains the reason for the four-gallon keg sent up from Melbourne. Any scroungers turning up at the sheep wash were evidently given short shrift.

On 3rd. August Henry remarked he had received a letter from Mr. Wedge, now married to Miss Wills, the Nixon children's governess. It is nice to know that the ship-board romance of those two middle-aged people – which had been derided by the youthful Henry at the time – should eventually have reached a happy conclusion. It is interesting, too, that he should give some further information about the Archdeacon and gives his name as Marriott.

This letter contains a list copied from his diary of Henry's correspondence since his arrival in Australia. The dates given show how long it took to receive mail from the old country and to send letters home. There is an inference here that the infamous Mr. Vivian was a man of the Cloth, a fact which Henry considered shielded him unfairly from the censure he deserved for his reprehensible treatment of Augusta, the girl to whom he was betrothed. Of course there is now no means of learning the full particulars of what had occurred in this context.

The latter part of this letter to his mother consists largely of a lengthy dissertation about the pros and cons of taking up the life of a sheep farmer in the outback. Although at this stage quite content with his lot and happy to report an all round improvement in the sheep market, Henry did not yet foresee his own ultimate success, when after twenty years of hard work and careful management, he was able to leave Australia for good, a wealthy man at a comparatively early age. He was emphatic about colonial conditions in the eighteen-forties being wholly unsuitable for the rest of the family to contemplate and afforded no prospect of marriage for his unattached sisters. In this respect there was to be a marked change within the next ten years. Two of his cousins from Dartmouth, sisters of "dear Gussie", were to come out on a visit in the early 'fifties and both found suitable husbands almost immediately – each of the young women being at that time around thirty years old and therefore probably considered to be destined for spinsterhood in Victorian England. William, however, decided Australia was not to be his choice and he went to India instead. He was to change his mind later on and eventually settled in Victoria in 1857, remaining there for the rest of his life.

Gobur. Goulbourne. Port Phillip.
July 14th. 1844

I cannot select a better day for the beginning of a letter to you, beloved Mother, than your birthday – trusting it has pleased God to spare you for the return of it in every health and earthly happiness – and that he may continue his blessings here, and finally crown you with true joy in heaven hereafter is the fervent prayer of your affectionate and dutiful as well as grateful son Henry; on the reflection of all that has been done for me, and when meditating on my present happy situation and the luxuries by which I am surrounded, I cannot sufficiently express my feelings of gratitude to Parents who have mutually sacrificed so much personal comfort in favour of each and all their children. May we manifest the effects of your good teaching and example by a steady, honest and godly life, remembering that the tie of duty, affection and gratitude to you is but loosed by death – 'Tis neither absence nor age can do away with it in my humble opinion, some may differ with me, but such is my persuasion and such, God grant, may be my rule of action.

We are verily in the midst of winter now, and the creek which heretofore has been mentioned as being a succession of ponds, or waterholes, is now a continued strong stream, looking like a little river in front of my hut. Our rain is heavy and constant and I am wet-footed from morning till night. Nothing like having waterproof boots and gaiters – mine were both, I fear, left at home, for I had no idea of such wet in Port Phillip, no more had my Father, since I well recollect him saying "What will be the use of these things?" when you were about packing up those macintosh leggings which have been frequently worn on horseback. A few pair of such as my Welsh boots would be invaluable now, since I have only those few light ones made by Ballman. However we may, I think, consider ourselves half through winter. The trees retain their foliage all the year, but grass looks the greenest towards the spring.

Nearly a month has elapsed since I penned this, so I will retrace my steps and give my journal from the above date, but I know not when it can go since at this time of year there are seldom any vessels for England.

15–16th. Nothing extraordinary but constant heavy rain.

17th. Gobur creek – or it might now be called a river – is flooded. It has washed away a bridge that I put across it with Mr. Fry's assistance. Ducks are very plentiful – I constantly have a roast. I have shot the greater part of them out of my hut window. I had two visitors, hunters, and an Honourable Mr. Kennedy! younger brother of the Marquis of Ailsa, who will of course succeed to that title. He seems very conceited, but we must not however form opinions on first sight.

18th. Had an unpleasant wet ride in a strange direction with no track for some distance having ridden about 32 miles to try and borrow some tobacco: for my complaining men would sooner lose a meal than a smoke.

19th. Rain, rain for ever! "Ranger" my hut-keeper's Kangaroo dog is a "non pareil". He kills kangaroo for me any day. I ride out with him and after having killed will bring me to his game if 3 or 4 miles off – the same day or any succeeding days. Few dogs will do so here.

21st. Cold southerly wind, & hopes of a change in the weather. My Sundays are generally spent in reading suitable books, and then writing.

22nd. A beautiful day after hard white frost. Employed today in the re-erection of Gobur bridge, which I flatter myself is now a workmanlike affair and warranted flood-proof as time will show. Previously I was wet so often in crossing the creek that it was not worth while to change.

23, 24, 25th. Fine days with sharp frosts at night.

26th. Busy firing and felling trees that obstruct my dray road – one tree I was crosscutting by moonlight, it fell in a water-hole, the noise of its fall and the splash in the water was truly a fine sight – it was a huge tree.

27th. I skinned a beautiful glossy black-bird – called here a Satin bird. Its eyes were bright blue.

29th. Fine. Sowing turnip, lettuce, cabbage & onion seed. Having lost a young dog in the Bush while running a kangaroo, I asked Fry to lend me his mare to try and find him – my own two were away. He, colonial-like, would not oblige, so to my great aversion I had to trudge it on foot, wading through creeks. When he refused me I merely said "Is this the return for the kindness I have shewn you?" and his conscience afterwards stung him – and he made up his mind to be no more dependent on me for bread – he in a few days leaves here for good (or more probably for bad) since he is simple and easily imposed on. Oh how true it is and pity 'tis, 'tis true that the more one does for these colonists, the less thanks one gets.

30th. Foggy morning. My horse being too fresh I took the spirit out of him by a day's Kangaroo hunting. What a number of bargains I could have got in sheep, cattle and horses had my £1000 been "in banco". I could have bought 500 wethers at 2/- per head which would have almost cleared the purchase money by first shearing time – and in two years have got perhaps 6/- or 8/- per head – their wool having paid off shepherds' wages &c. I have seen to my mortification many such-like purchases – where a child could not fail to see a profit – and Mr. Fry's mare was sold for £14. I would have bought her had the ready been forthcoming. I certainly came here at a very favourable time, had my pecuniary circumstances been more so. I am however very well pleased with my present investment, small as it is. Had Willie made up his mind to this queer solitary and uncouth life, he could have not done better than come with me. Times were at their worst, plenty of stations and runs in the market, which now are eagerly sought for, and to show the improvement in the value of a run – a neighbour of mine has sold his run, station and implements – without a single head of stock for £300, nearly all I gave for mine with the addition of 1243 sheep. (It is Snodgrass's station about 26 miles below me.)

The Goulbourn used to be the leading and *flash* district. Every station has changed hands but *one* – and the owner called at Gobur a day or two back and was dilating upon the melancholy reflections of being here as it were "the last of the Mohicans", and saying that Mamas at home had no occasion to caution their sons *now* against settling on the Goulbourn (for of a truth they had done so) since they are now "a pack of screws"! were his words – doubtless he included present company. Afterwards he said "With two or three exceptions." The settlers were, he said, a sort of clan and were always together known by the dreadful name of the "Goulbourn Mob" who used to carry everything before them, defying constabulary power and every other thing – poor fellows! thought I – What is their satisfaction now or advantage gained, homeless and friendless they are like wandering spirits – some going to England, other existing where they can. They may truly sigh and say "Tempora mutantur, et nos mutamur in illis".! Smoking, drinking and whist playing their only Bush occupations.

31st. Fine day. "Ranger" killed me a Kangaroo and brought me to it as in "Nine times by the taper's light" etc. I have luck and brought the Kangaroo on my lusty shoulder home, my horse carrying us both. You may wonder and say "Why, Harry seems to have nothing but Kangaroo hunting to do." but I omit mentioning any trivial circumstances – knowing such very minute detail would be uninteresting. I certainly have a little more leisure for other occupations as my sheep are all about 4 miles away at my out station – but then I go twice and sometimes thrice a week with flour &c. to observe that they get fair play. Other days I am grinding, digging, grubbing, carpentering – of which I am now very fond, having (thanks to Uncle Francis) such a superior tool chest, for were I idle and my mind unemployed now that I am alone I might begin to feel miserable and dislike the life. I know not a station where there is only one being living in solitary grandeur as I am. When visitors come they say "I could never live like you – I should hang myself or smoke myself mad". etc. I always laugh and say "You have no resources in yourself and you are too idle to work." – therefore to such people Bush life must be miserable.

1st. August. Rode to Darlows on the Devil's River and back to return an auger, and met the Carrier from Melbourne who had according to order some blankets for me, seed oats, and a keg of Rum, 4 gallons!! for my washing time. Visitors will soon come now like eagle Hawks hovering over their prey – for the word *grog* carries great weight with it in the Bush. They may come and they may expect, but trust me, they won't get any.

2nd. Fry and his chaps are gone for good, or more probably Bad. He by his meanness lately has greatly lowered himself in the estimation of men as well as master. He so vexed me at last that I said "Now, Fry, I tell you my mind, and I say it to your face that I need not be ashamed to say it behind your back: you are a mean, shabby, ungrateful man." What he was guilty of to raise such a speech from me is not worth detailing. Those few things that I wrote to accompany mine, for him I hope have not been sent, or being so, *I* shall detail and refund you.

3rd. I got a letter from Mr. Wedge (my fellow passenger) apologising for not having answered two of mine previously and saying he was getting frequent wiggings from his better half (Miss Wills) for not writing. He writes me: "7th June /44. In this colony (van Diemans Land) every class in the community is alike suffering from the continuance of the depression which pervaded the Colony when you were here, and instead of any hope of amendment, the position of the Colonists is getting worse and worse, and the Government – or rather Lord Stanley, is doing all he can to keep our noses to the grindstone, by his orders for the employment of the prisoners in the cultivation of the soil, not only for their own support, but to compete with us in the markets – so that all we can do is to grin and bear it. You may bless your stars that you were not induced to remain in this Colony."

Now if anyone advocates the cause of emigration to Tasmania in preference to the wide field of enterprise offered in our Colony (P.P.) read them the words of a bona fide old settler, and at the same time condemn not nor regret your own son's choice, but thank God with me that by his merciful guidance I have been safely led through all dangers, doubts and difficulties. Mr. W. also informs me that Archdeacon Marriott is returned to England on an important mission connected with the Church – if he has not been very much pressed for time, he is such a considerable kind-hearted person he would doubtless call at Pennsylvania. I think I mentioned in Maria's that Mr. Breton is married to a Miss D'Arch. Young Bear writes me word of the loss of the "Isabella" – fortunately no lives were lost – the mail, however, was – and it contained, he thought, "one of my letters." It might have been more, however to make it satisfactory to you I will again transmit my list of payments and receipts. The last letter of mine of which I have been assured of its coming to hand was to my Father from Launceston, Aug./43, and it is pleasant to me to know that up to that letter all have safely come to hand. Now if there was only one sent per Isabella, I'm afraid my dear Father's of June 24th. must be the wrecked one. Boyd took Maria's (with a portrait of a blackfellow) to Melbourne, and John's – and Cumming took Adelaide's and Maria's. Father's I sent per post to town. Let me know the result.

To	Will:	15th. Nov./43				
"	Mother	20. Dec. "				
"	John Smith	" "				
"	Father (by Sydney)	18 Jan./44				
	"	25 " "				
"	Genl. Boles	24 Feb:/44				
To	Gussie	24 Feb:/44			Received	
"	Mother	" "	From	Maria & Emily	14 Oct./43	
"	Alice (view)	" "	"	do. (no.2)	27 "	
"	Maria	" "	"	Louisa	" "	
"	Emily	" "	"	Mother	15 Nov.	
"	Louisa	27 March/44	"	Father	"	
"	Mr. Powell	" "	"	Mother	15 Jan/44	
"	Adelaide (view)	May 29th/44	"	Emily		
"	Maria	" "	"	Ady, Alice		
"	Father June	24/44	"	dear Gus		Dated
"	Maria (with black fellow)		"	Maria	May 29/44	2 Nov./43
		June 31/44	"	Maria		17 Jan/44
"	John	" "	"	Mother		5 Oct/43
			"	Mother	June 24/44	25 Dec/43

Thus it stands today Aug. 17th. /44

I often think with feelings of pain the conduct of Mr. Vivian. I am
persuaded it is providential interference for Gussie's welfare – and there are
yet happy days in store for her. How good and truly charitable does my
beloved Father always show himself in cases of real distress and emergency.
It was kind of him to bring dear Gus away from Dartmouth at such a time.
I cannot express the feelings of horror that pervaded me in reading the
account of it in Augusta's letter. I have perused it over and over again. His
gown shelters him from much, or I trust not her brother John would have
done something to convince him of the injury and affront he has committed.

If Willie makes up his mind to the Squatter's life in the Southern world
(as I have mentioned before and given my reasons for supporting it) I see no
use at all in his going to Mr. Powell's. The younger a person comes here, the
sooner he may expect to leave it and he is the better broken in to the life,
provided he has a sincere and honest friend in the Colony. Oh how rare a
character! All he would have to guard against would be making any too
intimate acquaintance on board ship. On his first landing let him stop at the
Prince of Wales Hotel and in the course of the following day call on Mr.
Bear – who though two years here is not *Colonial* (in my sense of the word)
and he will have the first opportunity of letting me know. This is only advice
should he intend coming. I know not even now whether I should prefer
India to this (except for the climate) and now that I have passed through
much anxiety of mind and vexation and I am rewarded by a quiet
comfortable home I am resolved not to alter my destination – "a rolling
stone gathers no moss" – says the old adage, but for one who had to choose
for himself as I had, I cannot, will not advise. I can only give my own
opinion of the life, and the country and I heartily thank my Father for his
repeated invitations home in case I regret my choice. Thank God – I am
contented and happy here – and see no cause for relinquishing my
occupation. But for the rest of my brothers I still say – there is plenty of
room in the liberal professions and the Indian Army for advancement and a
competency afterwards, and which is more suited to the substantial education which has been bestowed on us – for why should Major Godfrey's sons
seek to be more wealthy than Mr. Holroyd's, Doctor Mills' and the like?
After all by coming here roughing it and bushing it, penned up in a solitary
wooden hut, expecting to be better off for years of hard labour, privation
and toil – they find themselves probably not so independent as the above
mentioned youths without the same influence and standing in society. I
hope I may even in twenty years here be as well rewarded and have as
comfortable an income as my Father enjoys. Who is it that has retired from

this with a fortune? You can name no one at home – and I can hear of no one in the Colony – surely if squatting or sheepfarming is such an infallible role to independence, how is it one can find none that has made it? Out of the numbers that have come here there must have been some steady plodding fellows – no, be not deluded by books &c. Read this to Willie and let him know he may get as rich in India, apart from friends and relatives, where his music and drawing and other accomplishments serve only to amuse self. Civility and politeness thrown aside – sheep! – the main subject of this contemplation and occupation because to them he looks for bread. Let him ask himself could he fancy such a life in preference to the refinements and comforts of home or India! And the enjoyment of ladies' society, from which a man always reap advantage.

I truly pity him when that most annoying time shall arrive – I mean the important period of choosing his occupation – and deciding for himself what line of life would best suit his situation and prospects. My council *now* to him is "to pray earnestly to Almighty God for his divine guidance and assistance". It is since I made my own choice that God has been pleased to cast a light on my dark understanding and to make me know and feel through his Holy Spirit the efficiency of faithful and fervent prayer. *vide* 11 Mark 24.

I would *not* be one to advise any body to come here – much more a brother – for fear of future disappointment. I think you cannot accuse me of exhibiting only the bright and golden view of the question. I would say to all, I am contented and happy – but that is no reason why you must of consequence be so too. We are all of different dispositions. If a brother did come, I will take all care in my power of him and act a Brother's part. The country I have described, my own impressions of the life also – more I cannot say – except that the younger they come the better. Colonial management may be easily gained. John, I have positively dissuaded, having something at home and also a fixed habit on account of his years. In stronger terms again have I, and *do* I *still* dissuade you, my dear Parents from emigration. Melbourne is a miserably dull place, and in short – to use the words of a young lady (a neighbour of mine) "this country is not at all suited to ladies." Many are the constructions that may be put on that sentence – my own is there is no chance of a lady getting settled – the men are not in a condition to marry, for that is now the attainment of your daughters, or at least two of them.

Having just this moment a neighbour here on his way to Town, I will bring this to a hasty conclusion, excuse it – but opportunities of sending are rare from here, I send via Sydney to be sure of *going*. Love to all the

brothers, sisters and relatives and kindest remembrances to friends. My
dutiful affection to dear Father,

and believe me ever your dutiful
and loving son

Henry Godfrey.

There is a *great deal* in this letter since it is written close – and a large sized
sheet.

[Postmarked 7th. September 1844. Received Exeter 15th. February 1845 –
stamped.]

Another letter was started to his mother on October 2nd. Henry was then in
a depressed state of mind owing to the incessant heavy rains. The resulting
floods caused the death of many of his new-born lambs. Later on, however,
he learnt that other settlers had fared far worse than he had, sustaining
irreplaceable loss of stock by drowning.

He remarks he is using a quill pen instead of his usual steel nib. The
difference this made to his handwriting is quite noticeable – it is neater,
thicker and less scratchy than when he wrote with a metal pen nib. There
can be no doubt Henry enjoyed letter writing. To him it was a pleasure
rather than a duty – a means of expressing his thoughts and opinions to the
family now so far away with whom he had such a deep affinity. He admitted
when writing home he was able to express himself more freely and
spontaneously than when he had to write more formal letters to friends
outside the family circle. He did not allow his correspondence to interfere
with the many tasks he had to perform about the station, reserving his letter
writing for wet days or dark evenings when he wrote by the light of tallow
candles – those candles made from the mutton fat obtained by the
boiling-down process already mentioned.

Again he repeats his reasons for dissuading the family from emigrating,
all of which seemed sound common sense at the time.

Flora, whose forthcoming marriage his mother had evidently mentioned
to him in a letter she had written on 15th. March must have been a Scottish
housemaid in the Godfrey establishment at 5 Pennsylvania Park.

The allusion to his elder brother John – at that time 23 years old – implies
he was then engaged in business in Portugal. This explains why there is less
mention of him than of Henry's other brothers and sisters, all of whom were

still living at home. They all seem to have had some aptitude for drawing and painting as well as for music. Henry's own gifts in this respect were to bring him posthumous fame as will be seen in due course – something which would doubtless have astonished him greatly had he been able to have any inkling about it when he drew for his own amusement. At the time when he was writing in his hut at Gobur he regretted the lack of suitable subjects to sketch in Australia with its monotonous landscape of dense bush and forests of tall gum trees, though later on in another locality he was to find sufficient subjects to exercise his talent to no small extent.

It would seem Henry completely missed the point of his mother's remark about the two servant maids leaving the Godfrey household without having known him. This fact in itself was, of course, quite irrelevant – what she had implied was that the period during which the girls had been employed at No. 5 was shorter than the length of time Henry had been away from home, a time which to a fond mother would have seemed very long indeed. He must have been rather obtuse not to understand the implication behind her observation, especially as later on he quotes her as having said, "We are wearying to hear from you." This in itself is a clear indication of how much he was missed by his family in Exeter.

His advice to parents in general on the subject of alcoholic drink shows sound common sense and some psychological understanding – rather remarkable to have come from so young a man. No doubt his own parents had already laid the foundations for his views by the expression of their own strongly felt principles and the way they conducted the household management in their home. Henry himself was quite prepared to take a drink on appropriate occasions, but he was well aware of the dangers resulting from over-indulgence.

At the end of this letter Willie is censured for not writing to his elder brother who thought about him so much and who had written him two long letters in the course of the past year, hoping he would decide to join him out in Australia. Possibly the younger boy resented the sanctimonious and admonitary overtones used by the elder one in writing to him and he delayed replying because he was at a loss to know how to express his response.

Gobur. River Goulburn. Port Phillip.
October 2nd./44

Beloved Mother,

I find myself seized with a fit of (don't be frightened) letter writing! and there is none to throw a bucket of cold water on me – so I am afraid it will last beyond the usual length of time. I can only attribute this (to me) unnatural seizure to the doleful state of the weather & ergo my reflective & melancholy mood. You may judge that it fully amounts to a mania for I have positively perpetrated a letter to Louisa, Father & dear Gus, & am now commencing one to you in the incredibly short space of time of 8 days! though I have dated them differently. You may easily imagine the prospect from my wooden domicile is anything but an inducement to tempt me out of doors. My creek is flooded so tremendously with the late incessant heavy rains that my wheat paddock, tiny garden is under water – a great part of the newly erected horse paddock is also swept away. The poor bridge is completely out of sight – but these are trifling compared with the pecuniary loss I am sustaining by the deaths of every unfortunate little lamb that is being at this time ushered into the world. The first night 7 died – last night 22 & tonight (Oct. 1st.) as the rain continues – goodness knows how many will go. It is very disheartening to me, being my own first increase, & as 117 of them were carefully lambed down & well mothered till this unreasonable rain set in – but hold – I am proceeding too far. Why should I murmur at things over which I have no control – "It is the Lord, let him do what he seemeth good." Oh what sinners we are, dear Mother, how apt we are to murmur and be discontented if anything appears to us to go wrong – when we well know it is our duty & interest to be resigned and contented that what is, is for the best & if we *are* punished, it is not half so severe as our transgressions deserve. Instead of sitting & playing the violin (as my dear friend & master Mr. Powell used to do when the rain was pouring on his cut crops), having no violin to play on, I sit amusing myself with this sheet, every now and then looking at the open door to see whether the water actually means to walk into my hut or not.

I think by answering fully every query contained in two last received letters, (the one dated 8th. Febry. – the other 15th. March "to go by London Courier-Ship") I shall have abundant materials for filling this sheet, so as to make it tolerably legible, you may easily observe the difference of writing in this from my other letters lately written. I have a *quill* in hand now – they were *steel-penned*.

Doubtless it would have been a very advantageous thing for me in every way, could I have got the management of such a place as Col. Breton's on my immediate landing, But I never could have waited unemployed long enough to get his answer & consent out here – no, I do not at all regret that I have undertaken the responsibilities of an establishment of my own as times are. Even supposing I could not make it answer, as I stake little, I could but lose little – & having lost as little as possible before I did settle, I should be young enough to return in a year or two if it appeared things would not go right with me – but there is every reason to believe the contrary. Moreover, as I have written before – were I inclined to sell, I should *make* money, instead of losing by the transaction, so my Father need not think that money lost would be any obstacle or hindrance to my coming home – my spirit opposed the idea far more than anything else.

Your copy of correspondence between that reprobate Vivian & dear Gus was very acceptible to me. I perused it as soon as I got to my station, with feelings of pleasure & pain, but the former predominated since it may be well considered an escape from misery for so good a girl. You mention sending 3 newspapers directed to Mr. Breton at the same time as my Father's Sydney packet letter, the papers have not come to hand. However much my dear Daddy urges, *do not you* encourage the idea of emigration, it would be miserable for you all & as for my Father he could never exist in Melbourne, & the bush life would be too monstrous for him. Farming would never pay here, therefore his sons would all be scattered about squatting & seldom see home or each other, & my sisters would not see a soul, their playing, singing & every other accomplishment thrown aside (for one soon gets tired of playing to oneself.) It would be a pity to see a respectable (and we flatter ourselves *talented*) family dwindled & descended into squatters & colonists! You can hardly enter into the feeling of my aversion for the place owing to the stamp of people whom I have come across, & with whom I have had to do. For a young man, it is not much consequence, for if he comes here he may gain confidence and profit by the folly of others – or may act the contrary & turn wild, and then he will soon go to mischief. But to see the whole family sacrificed would be a pity, & God forbid I should ever be the cause of *your* coming here, or even anyone else – for it is not difficult from no selfish motive, for if I studied self, I should say come at once – never mind making 8 children wretched & unhappy in this lonely banished region for the sake of comfort & happiness of myself.

I feel quite concerned at the trouble & expence all my letter etc. must have been to the Bishop as well as Mr. Breton. I wrote to the former apologising for it – if you did the same it would not be amiss. You gave credit for a longer visit & for seeing more of the country in Tasmania, however it did not take me long to see that settling there was quite out of the question with my means, as well as for the poor prospect of success held out to all grain-growers. Had you directed Henry G., Port Phillip – to him at the Post Office, I should have had no difficult in getting them all , & without causing such trouble to my Van Diemans Land friends – but it will be all right for the future, you know how long before this – that my name with, care of Bear & son, or to be at the Post Office till called for, will always come to hand – for I told young Bear whenever there was an English arrival, or the overland mail from Sydney, to ask & pay postage if anything for me & to forward it at the first opportunity.

You say something about a present to the Bishop. I know of none that would please him more than some new work – if Mrs. Carlyon could take the trouble of selecting a work, I know no one so capable of guessing the episcopal taste – for he is very partial to a Library & it might be enclosed in any parcel sent by Mr. Woodcock – it would hardly be worth while to make it a parcel of itself. Any good collection of sacred music, or some approved book of sketches – they must be *new* – for he has almost every work you can name up to date of his embarkation. I am sorry that no opportunity offered me here of writing to the Cape to Mrs. Marshall (as I promised to do) One vessel only (the Lord Keane) was to touch at the Cape from this Port, all others preferring the Cape Horn Passage, and I had not a chance of getting a letter from the Bush when she sailed.

I congratulate Flora on her engagement & hope it may ere long become a match. She will make a "gude little wife."

To give the true answer to your question – I must confess the greater part of the Port Phillip Settlers have that peculiar manner of speaking through the nose – I have frequently observed it; they generally walk with a great stoop.

I now open and answer any thing contained in your letter of 15th. March, "per London" etc. The parcel I received safely, but curiously in Melbourne. It had not been previously opened so the contents must be all right, but being on horseback I was forced to leave all except the waistcoat (which I wore) in Town – and I thank you for it, dear Mother, as a neat & very acceptible present, quite in accordance with my present taste. It is long in the waist – like every thing else made for me – it can nevertheless be easily altered.

Though my Father seems so very anxious about the result of my undertakings, or rather of my outset – he is long ere this apprised of my favourable commencement & comfort in every way – except the want of some little money with which to make a start – and for which I wrote in January /44 as nearly all my cash was consumed in the purchase of the Station, horses & travelling from home – having but £500 that was available. I think I have done very well to be able to write so favourable an account before one year of settlement has elapsed, as both he & I (if truth be written) expected to feel disappointment, and perhaps discontent in my letters for 2 years at least. My reconcilliation to the strangeness of the country & the widely different mode of living and management to what I have been used, has by no means been a tardy one. Mr. Bear has supplied any cash that I may require till my remittance arrives, otherwise I should have been at a complete standstill. He certainly has been my only friend here & true adviser, sparing me all possible expense (just at this critical time) by keeping my horse, as well as myself whenever I have been in Melbourne. Had I not observed a strict economy at first, the Station would never have been mine – for it was my determination to spend as little as possible. When first I came to Melbourne & stopped at the Prince of Wales – I was there from the 14th. October till 16th. November, and my bill came to £7.15.6 at an hotel where the charge for Breakfast 2/-, dinner 3/6, Tea 2/- & bed 2/- per day came to 9/6, so with a little calculation you may see I was not *extravagant*, but many times walked away from the hotel at dinner time to get a dinner on sweets – accepting also every invitation. This is a little "entre nous", don't let *every body* read this piece of parsimony. Of course I would never do it but under the circumstances that I felt were those over which I had no control. I am letting you into a little of my *private* account book – pray make it not public.

I see by your letter Gussy has gone to pay a visit to Cheltenham. She will be sure to enjoy herself with such a nice person as Mrs. D. I hear Emily & Louisa & finally Gus are being photographed – how is it no mention is made of sending me a copy of one of them? I should like good portraits of them at *my expense*– and some of yourself, beloved Mother, to be sent in the first packet of goods. I honestly mean what I say – and trust me I'll pay you, not being quite Colonial in dealings though I am in manner – though they gave Louisa only *one eye*! I hope it was not in the middle of her forehead.

You say Henry Holroyd is come home to arrange some affairs for the House – perhaps some *domestic* one too. There is a singular and perfectly unintelligible passage in your letter to me – I quote it correctly: "Margaret & Elizabeth both gave warning today, the latter is really unfit for our situation, she suffers so much from her swelled leg – I cannot understand why Margaret left, but it is melancholy to think that not one of them knows *you*!"

The more I have endeavoured to understand the meaning of the latter part of this queer sentence, the more puzzling it has been to me – your thoughts must have been in Australia while your *pen* was in Pennsylvania. Why should it be melancholy that two servant maids never knew me? With your note of admiration or astonishment, if I gave you no *encouragement* in my letters from Tasmania for emigration, I am sure all those from Port Phillip would contain less of that ingredient, for the two evils I would say Choose the least & go to Van Diemans Land where there would be some respectable people in preference to this young colony. But I still & ever shall write "stop at home if you wish to be happy, and to conduce to the happiness of those children who are about you."

I had reason to be pleased with myself today (4th. Oct.) for having got 3 letters in readiness & only waiting to be sealed, since a neighbour Mr. Marshall (brother of the Emigration Marshall in London) called on his way to Town and gave me only just time to seal them & enclose to Bear, begging him to send them via Sydney if there was no vessel from Port Phillip, one to Father (17th. Sept.) Louisa (20th.) & Gussy (10th.) dated. I hope they may reach – and in truth I do more than hope, I expect – for it is no use to sit down & write about such feelings of doubt & despair as you by your own letters do evince about their non arrival. I write as if convinced that your dear eyes will certainly peruse this. You say, "we are wearying to hear from you." Surely there can be no great interval between the receipt of all my letters – for the stream of them is kept up, as soon as one is dispatched another is commenced. In fact young Bear who posts them all writes me word thus: "I should think you have not much to do, on account of the English letters you write." But I told him they were all written with the aid of mutton fat, or else on a very rainy, suicidal-sort of day, of which we have had no scarcity lately, which fully accounts for this flow of letter scribbling. I do not see any occasion for directing my letters (via Sydney) to the care of Mr. Jos. H. Willis – for as letters have heretofore come to Melbourne, without being paid in Sydney, why should they not continue to do so? I am not informed on the point, but as soon as I know you shall be made aware of it – in the interim however for safety's sake I'll comply with the direction of writing to the above named individual in Sydney.

I have had the Blacks here lately, and though they have robbed an outstation of one of my neighbours, they seemed to be peacefully inclined towards me, as the following little dialogue between me and the chief will prove. You will hardly understand it, but it will amuse you. Black: "You come quamby here?" Self: "Yes." Black: "Where Missa Bide?" (alias Boyd, whose station this was.) Self: "He gego Melbourne." Black: "Budgery you? Plenty bugana (beef). Big one sugar. Big one Damper?" Self: "Borack, no good, Black fellow." upon which he only retaliated "No good whitefellow." And though I gave him no Grub we parted good friends shaking hands – short but sweet, containing nothing alarming.

So Johnny has been up the Douro again, he must by this time be quite au fait at the taste of various wines. Doubtless he had made some pretty sketches, unless his time has been much occupied with *business*, that comprehensive & conclusive word. I wrote him the letter end of June last. For my part I felt much disappointed in the unvaried feature of the landscape in this Colony – if one view is taken you have nearly all Port Phillip. There is very little food for the artist, either in a *pecuniary* or pencil-iary point of view. The Ornithologist on the other hand has a very wide & varied field for the execution of his pursuit, since there appears to be different birds on almost every different creek. Webster & myself about ten miles apart have each birds that are never seen on the other's run, & so it seems all over the country. I'm afraid this last paragraph will act as a sort of spur to the bent of my dear Father's inclination (which is for emigration). It is hardly worth blotting out now that it is written.

What vocal evenings we shall have – please God I ever live to return, my voice will back against Maria's for *strength*, though not for *flexibility*. (And though I say it that should not *sing* it) I can give as loud a coo-ee as most others. I shall have to take lessons again on the violincello of Willie if he does ever come here.

I heard a piece of news today which raised the hero of it (a friend of mine) some little in my estimation. viz. that Cumming had publicly in broad day broken a whip over our late M.C.'s shoulders (Mr. Ebden) for a thing that he deserved even worse treatment than that – for unsealing & perusing some of Cumming's letters with the care of which he was entrusted to Sydney! Behold in this *refined* community of Port Phillip what our Honourable & Learned Mr. Ebden can be guilty of! What responsible family would emigrate? Though Cumming has taken the dust out of his coat, he can never take the conceit out of his carcase. His pride is doubtless a peg lower.

I saw Wrey in town the last time – he was suffering from bad eyes & had made them no better by making the wash of sulphate of lime & water *too* strong. He talked of going in about a fortnight to some appointment he had got in the Cressy Estate (belonging to a company) in Tasmania – but it is as likely as otherwise that I shall see him crawling about Melbourne when I am in Town with my wool. Poor fellow, I feel much for him, and greatly blame those who sent him away, knowing of what delicate materials his constitution is composed. What Cumming is going to do I know not, he talked last of going in company with some others to some unexplored country towards "Wimmera" taking cattle – but he is always talking of a move. They will require their Pistols if they go far that way.

Now that I have spent one year here (at least within a few days) I will tell you in what my expectations were realised or disappointed regarding climate – but mind you, no two years are alike here, so that this could not be deemed fair criticism or average. It is undoubtedly a healthy climate, that is if we are to judge it by our own ailments & the complaints of others, which are in the aggregate few indeed through all the heat of the summer and the incessant rain of winter, I have not felt one day's illness since I came to Port Phillip. There is far more rain than I anticipated, and one's warm clothing is required even more than at home, because the heat of summer is far greater than that of a summer in England. We are all very chilly mortals, any day without sunshine seems to us very cold, for there is a pleasure in the enjoyment of an Australian Spring Day which no pen can describe.

My trifling loss of about 30 lambs during this flood shrinks to insignificance since I heard from neighbours whose flock of 800 wethers with their fleeces on were washed away, hurdles and all by the tremendous rise of the River Goulbourn. They are 3 or 4 brothers of the name of Brown, and very hard-working, persevering fellows. Another neighbour also lost his cart laden with stores of wheat, tea & sugar, all from Melbourne. The bullocks were fortunately released from it. I hear it has been the highest flood on the Goulbourn in the recollection of white people. Mr. Marshall has had two feet of water in all his buildings, and a Mr. McClean at the Devil's River has been completely turned out with five feet of water in his home station! So much for the folly of building head stations in a low spot, near a creek or river merely for the sake of having a short water carriage in summer, which was a mistake under which all the lazy early settlers laboured. The site of Gobur was well chosen by Boyd, being quite close to water for summer use and above the reach of any flood in winter.

On the 6th. October I thought of and prayed for my dear Father. His health was drunk by myself and a neighbour in some Rum which had been procured by me for washing time, on such a day I could not but tap the keg. While talking of spirits – this is a bit of advice that a youngster like myself does venture to offer Parents generally. Never prohibit your sons from having a free use of wine & spirits (in season) when at home – at the same time teaching them by precept, and pointing out to them by example the harmful effects and sure misery & ruin that must attend a habitual excess of liquor. All settlers (they are few indeed) with whom I have conversed on the subject & who like myself have not the least particle of love for liquor, attribute it, in some measure, to their never having restrictions placed upon them under their Parents roof – whereas those who are never allowed a drop but on a birthday and from whom the decanter was locked away directly Dinner was over, when they leave the watchful eye & kind roof of the

Parents are sure to become an easy prey to men of wild habits and dissipated modes of living.

I must bring this scribble to an end, as I will not attempt to cross so closely and badly written a letter, but will continue my journal to Maria as I have lately written to Louisa & Em: as well as dear Gus. How is it Mister William or W. Godfrey Esquire does not write a line to his distant brother? I have written him two long letters, both of which have fortunately come to hand. Remember me kindly to *all* my friends, as well as my friend & quondam Pastor. Give love & kisses to dear Father and all my sisters & brothers. May the gracious Lord bless you all.

I am dear Mother until death
your dutiful & loving Henry Godfrey.

P.S. On 23rd. Nov./44 I received your letter of March 13 per "Augustina" also one from dear Aunt Ann & from Maria & Emily (jointly) of March 29th. Pie's 6th letter. I shall send shortly to Emily & one to Father acknowledging his remittance lately received. In haste, H.G.
N.B. Send me word whether this my 6th. letter to you has come to hand, as well as all intermediate ones for I seem to myself to enter into detail in every letter to you. This is the longest letter sent home, if I mistake it not. H.G.

The letter Henry wrote to his father bearing the date December 2nd. 1844 consists of a very large folded sheet completely over-written crosswise with a fine steel nib. A magnifying glass was found to be helpful in deciphering it. Addressed to his father, in this letter Henry thanked him for the remittance sent by Banker's Order. The sum in question freed him from all anxiety regarding his current money matters. He was also relieved to learn of his parents' change of heart about insisting on the young man's return home, something which had evidently been on the cards if his prospects had shown no signs of improving. Henry was now able to assure them that things had changed greatly for the better and the success of his future prospects seemed definitely assured.

He was still thinking about the possibility of William emigrating within the next few years. In the event of the two brothers joining forces, Henry said there would be no need for the younger to have a preliminary training in farm management with Mr. Powell in South Wales as he himself had done. He was now sufficiently experienced to impart all necessary advice.

His friend Cummings was planning to set up a Station with a partner in the remote outback region between the Wimera and Glenelg rivers some two hundred miles west of Melbourne beyond the Grampian range – at that time a virtually unexplored area. He was well aware these two men were likely to encounter many unforeseen difficulties and dangers in this wild terrain where their chances of success were by no means certain. It would be interesting to know how they fared and what became of them, but there seems to be no way of finding out.

Within the next few years Henry himself was to venture into largely unknown territory which was almost as far from civilisation as where these other settlers had gone, though in quite another direction. No hint that this move was contemplated is given in any of the surviving letters written while he was living at Gobur.

at Mr. Bear's
Collingwood.
December 2nd /44

Beloved Father,

My first clip of wool being on the road to Melbourne, I am just arrived from the Bush to sell it & purchase another twelvemonths stores; I do not recollect when I have felt so overjoyed as on my arrival to find 5 English letters for me containing the three sets of Drafts, which of course were directly shewn & accepted at the Bank, though not payable for 33 days. What can I say? What return can I make, dearest Father, for your goodness in sending me the requested remittance with *such dispatch*, and that after having sent a letter which I acknowledge to have received urging, even commanding me to leave this country – just a short time before. That letter caused me more anxiety than you can well imagine fearing lest you would retain the money to ensure my return. Only ten months elapsed between my letter for it & the receipt of yours. I call that very quick work. On opening your letter dated 18th. June & sent per "Lord Aukland", I find you in a great bustle & packing off for Dartmouth. I will however reply to anything in it that you would wish to be informed of. I am very glad that you so kindly considered the position I should have been in had the money not arrived in the estimation of any who might chance to have been my creditors, and I am also glad that you recall your mandate for my immediate return – it was written upon the best of motives, and through affectionate desire to release me from those *apparent* miseries and un-propitious prospects, to which you gave yourself credit for hastening me, but thank God I am enabled now to write a very different account of the state of things and my prospects generally. And I have every reason to thank you for your advice and commend your foresight in sending me to this country just at the *very time* I did come, though against the will & wish of all my relatives & friends – but who can advise like a Father? – especially when that Parent's trust is reposed in his God.

I am sorry that my earlier letters from Melbourne should have been of such a doleful nature as to cause you the least anxiety of mind, but every allowance was to be made for my arrival in a strange & friendless country where those whom I expected to find prosperous were not in a position to assist me, but rather to ensnare me. The state of things here is much brightened since I came, then the tide was at its lowest ebb, whereas now it is fast rising & on a surer basis than on the quicksand of credit, bills & huge discounts on which the seeming prosperity of the colony then rested. The Banks now allow us interest, so money *must* be invested, every one's credit is known – rogues who were driving their carriages in the growing time of trickery have now found their level & obliged to pay. The boiling-down system lately adopted has been the saving of the Colony, sheep will now be always of some standing value and these last accounts of wool have completely crowned the whole and totally altered the Settlers' prospects, whose labour must now be amply rewarded, if slowly, yet *surely*, when accompanied with prudence & perseverence. Wool is bought of the settlers now quickly at 1/2d. per pound. How different from last year when it was varying from 8d. to 10d. Even let it fall & keep at 1/- per pound, – those who have bought clean sheep at anything under 10/- a head must do very well.

You seem by your letter to fancy that Gobur is a farm – be not so mistaken. It is only the squatting station of H. Godfrey Esquire who pays £10 per annum for the use of the land to her most Gracious Majesty Victoria. When you hear of me buying land here you may think me *married* or *mad*. The one is as probable as the other. This letter will appear to you suddenly contradictory to all I have before written about prospects, but it is not more sudden than the change in the times from bad to good. I still maintain I do not like Colonial dealings, or people, nor would I ever wish to have you all here, yet I hope in a few years to be able to return to visit you all. I can see my way now pretty clearly & calculate the probability of success which before these accounts of the value of wool & tallow came I was not quite clear about. I used to think whatever can be done with all the wethers of the fast increasing flocks in Port Phillip. Melbourne cannot consume the meat, and they must be comparatively valueless, but now we resort to the *boiler* to get rid of surplus stock – and wool is ever of value. If they do moreover export to China we shall do well! Cattle have fallen in my estimation lately as an investment for Capital, you get nothing off their bones, no yearly return as with wool.

You seem anxious about Willie & give the subject for my consideration, to which I hasten to reply – but of course I particularly abstain from giving advice or cause to persuade him. I write *you* what is the state of things here and what I will do for him if he comes. The life he knows already to be a rough one, let him therefore choose for himself. More can be done here with money (by a young man) than at home in any profession, but the temptations to dissipation and vice are far greater. If therefore a youth has not the steadiness, let him not think for one moment of coming here – he comes to his grave. The times being fast in the rise, are not so good for a beginner as when I came, for now I can see it in that light; nevertheless I think I might be supported by saying that, come when he will, any *steady* young man will be worth some money here before he would have gained anything like the same quantity in England. But then he loses society, all pleasure & luxuries, for merely the bare necessities of life, for anxiety, toil and solitude. There is not the least occasion for his going to Mr. Powell, for all he would require to know could be learnt here.

The earlier a youth comes the better, if he has a real friend in the Colony – otherwise let him cut his wisdom teeth, and he will even then be "picked up". Of course he would never want a home or even the best advice that I could give, or get for him. I bought sheep & all at 6/- per head. I could easily now sell at 10/-, perhaps 12/- per head and when I bought, my number was 1243. I now own 1979 and have had £179 worth of wool off them. A proof of the rise in the value of sheep, & the good fortune attending my first small but good investment, not having invested a twelvemonth.

I have just received my Mother's September Packet letter in which she sends the list of things contained in my promised box – saddle etc. I am sorry you should have parted with the last bottle of Curry Powder for me. I could have waited very patiently for it. I feel anxious about the arrival of my Case. The "Lord Ream" is overdue – it will, I dare say, be here about the middle of February. I need not say how delighted I shall be to open it and welcome the imported contents. If on any other occasion you are sending me a Box or case, you could ask Mrs. Lee if there was anything that could be forwarded to Mrs. Bear – and it would be a trifling return for their kindness and hospitality to me. When staying at their Cottage I spend very musical evenings – at least Piano and voice, and this last time got my violincello up, it is generally kept at Dr. Sanford's – but I do not play with any satisfaction to myself from want of practice, so singing is more in request.

I saw Cummings yesterday (January 15th. /44) and he took me to an Inn where he is stopping and insisted on reading to me Mr. Holroyd's last three letters to him. He also shewed me a Power of Attorney that he was just about to send home to Mr. Holroyd over some estate of his or his Aunt's. It was witnessed by two parties here, but if I recollect rightly it was not signed by a Notary Public which is I believe a *sine qua non*. If I see him again before he sends, I intend mentioning it to him. It seems his relative Mrs. Egerton has honoured his draft for £1000, which has put him in far better spirits & circumstances than he has enjoyed for some time. His plans are at last cut out. He has taken a number of sheep of a Sir J. Peddar on terms (about 3000.) The terms I do not quite know. Whether it may be managing them for a third of the wool and increase or a half or what, I cannot say. However he found a run about 200 miles from Melbourne between the "Wimmera" and Glenelg Rivers, and has got a Partner in the concern called Carter – this person having money to pay all expenses at least the first year. When I told Cumming what I know and heard about Carter – being rather fast and flash in Town – he said he would never have joined, but merely because he literally had no ready money resources himself wherewith to carry on a station. I expect he will meet with much annoyance and risk from the Blacks up there – and of course it will be tremendous up-hill work for him, poor fellow. Too good a heart, and putting his name on other people's papers was his ruin, but I hope he will now give up all his bad associates and habits and begin on a fresh footing. He seems quite inclined to do so. He constantly said to me, What a lucky fellow you are, Godfrey, to have come when you did – to have found such a friend and adviser as Mr. Bear – and to have the advantage of living with a quiet family like his, – and keeping yourself away from Town associates and expenses, which – unless a man keeps himself perfectly steady and quiet – are the stepping stones to ruin.

I must now bring this to a close as I am just off for the Bush – promising to write another very shortly from thence. I offer my kindest remembrances to all friends at home, to each & all of our dear Family as well as my Mother.

And believe me,

Your ever affectionate and dutiful

little

Henry Godfrey.

5

Boort

The last letter we have from Henry while he was still at Gobur was written in December 1844. In it, as we have seen, there was no indication that he was contemplating a move within the next few months, yet it is known he had settled in quite another part of the country some time during the following year, though the first existing letter relating to his changed circumstances is dated Christmas Day 1846.

The spot destined to be Henry Godfrey's home off and on for the next eighteen years and his brother Frederic's for even longer lay 140 miles to the north-west of Melbourne in an area first seen by white men barely ten years earlier. In 1836 when the explorer Sir Thomas Mitchell and his party gazed over the level landscape from the summit of one of the few hills in the region – a granite-capped outcrop later to be known as Pyramid Hill on account of its shape – they saw a vast expanse of rough grassland interspersed with patches of dense scrub and forests of tall gum trees towering above the undergrowth. Sir Thomas envisaged the potential development of this land for farming and stock rearing. At that time it was the haunt of kangaroos and many species of smaller marsupials, while the human inhabitants were the tribes of Aborigines leading self-sufficient lives with the dingo dogs they had introduced many centuries before when they had first populated the great southern continent from the islands to the north.

During the next few years, directly after Mitchell and his expedition had first set eyes on what was to become north-west Victoria, settlers had gradually infiltrated the area from the south and had begun to set up sheep and cattle stations. Trees were felled and the bush cleared by burning so as to provide land suitable for agriculture and open pasture where sheep could graze. The only access was, of course, by horseback, while heavy goods were conveyed in ox-drawn drays over a trackless countryside intersected by rivers and creeks which in the rainy season became raging torrents apt to flood the low-lying surrounding land, while in other places the way was barred by impenetrable woodland.

In 1845 Henry Godfrey obtained a tract of 180 square miles of grassland and bush from Mr. Bear whose son Tom was managing an adjacent run to

84

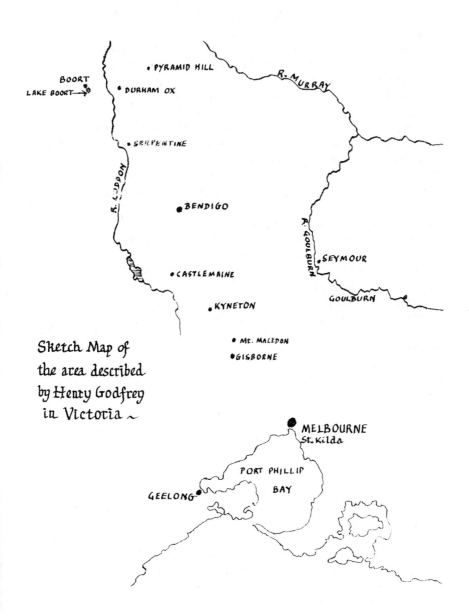

Sketch Map of
the area described
by Henry Godfrey
in Victoria ~

the south-west known as the Serpentine. Pyramid Hill was twenty-six miles
to the north-west. The area was watered by the river Loddon, a tributary of
the Murray, flowing almost directly due south, while parallel to it on the
east flowed the Serpentine Creek. The land Henry was to control adjoined
the Fernihurst Station in the south, situated at the junction of Keningapule
Creek with the Loddon river. This creek emptied its waters into a huge
swamp surrounded by trees – box, pine and numerous kinds of gum
predominating – and teeming with many species of duck and other wild
birds. Beyond the marshy area a hill stood silhouetted against the sky. It
was of no great height, but in a flat region any sort of eminence appeared
significant and thus this was the spot where the natives lit their signalling
fires, directing the columns of smoke to indicate messages to their comrades
on the plains beyond. Their word for smoke was 'Boort' and this was the
name Henry chose for his new station.

It would be interesting to know what were Henry's first impressions of the
place that was to be his home and where later he was to bring his wife and
children to reside for more than ten years, but unfortunately no letters have
been preserved after the end of 1849.

To reach Boort from Melbourne took three days on horseback when
conditions were favourable – and that was not by any means always the
case. The traveller had to cross rivers or creeks, contend with floods in wet
weather and in the hot dry summer he was obliged to ride in a cloud of red
dust churned up by his horse's hooves from the rough surface of the track.
There were a few hostelries at certain spots within the reach of civilisation,
but it was often necessary to camp overnight in the bush. In due course
Henry was fortunate in being able to break the journey at Mount Ridley
near Macedon, the home of his cousin Augusta and her husband Captain
James Pearson who settled there in 1847.

By the time he wrote the first of the extant letters from Boort Henry was
quite comfortably established in a wooden house close to the swampy lake.
There were huts for his employees, and outbuildings had been erected for
use as wool sheds and for carpentry purposes. Subsequently his dependable
overseer, McWhirter, was to have his own quarters and the main homestead
became a substantial dwelling with brick chimneys and a wide verandah
encircling the steeply pitched roof. Even as early as 1846 he had a garden
producing fruit and vegetables and he was growing oats to provide food for
his horses, while he hoped to harvest wheat successfully in the future after
the failure of his initial crop.

In the letter written on Christmas Day he refers to others he has
dispatched to his sisters containing all his recent news – sadly, these have

not survived. But the one we have, brief though it is, has plenty in it of interest – not least describing as it does the perils of the lonely life he was leading when a tumble from his horse in crossing a river could so easily have had fatal consequences. He soon discovered a sizeable stretch of water some ten miles north of his homestead and learnt it was known as Lake Leāghur. The land beyond this point was farmed by a man named John McMillan with whom he found himself at odds regarding the ownership and rights of the property in that area. His opinion of McMillan in particular and of Scotsmen in general was far from flattering. This enmity continued over a period of several years until the dispute relating to the boundary was finally settled to the satisfaction of both men. It is worth noting here that McMillan and his descendants continued farming at Leāghur long after Henry Godfrey and his brother had left Boort, and there is a representative of the family still living in the district today.

The young man's description of Christmas spent all alone indoors contains no hint of self-pity for his solitary plight. On the contrary, he was glad to be able to relax by himself without being concerned about his stock and he enjoyed a traditional meal prepared for him in the kitchen – though he must have found it rather odd having a Christmas dinner in the middle of the summer season. It is to be hoped the person responsible for making the excellent plum pudding was allowed to have a good share of it even though he was not invited to eat at the owner's table. In the Bush the rigid rules governing Victorian class distinction appear to have been observed just as firmly as back home in the old country, but at the same time hospitality and shelter were readily granted to any lonely traveller in the wilds of Australia.

As this letter bears no signature it looks as if a second sheet is missing.

Boort, Loddon.
Xmas Day 1846

My very dear Father,

Having but lately written three or four letters home I fear my little store of news is pretty well exhausted, nevertheless having the will I shall doubtless find the way of filling this sheet with detail of some description. My last letters were to Louisa and Maria each on their respective birthdays. On the second of Dec. I was hard at work mowing my oat crop – for my overseer was ignorant of the use of the scythe, and I had no man on the station who could do it; it was a very warm morning and in the afternoon we were relieved by a tremendous fall of rain, thunder & lightning – I finished on the 4th. On the 5th. I rode to see how Dunsford was getting on with his shearing and found there two English letters awaiting my perusal, one from Mother, 30 July & from Maria dated 15th. July, Hereford.

On the 6th. when riding bareback to fetch in two of our runaway horses, they took to the Lodden being closely followed by me – my horse would not be stopped but plunged in after them & he being unable to get a footing when galloping through the stream, he caught his legs in a hidden log & gave himself and his rider as pretty a somersault & ducking as we would wish to have. He fell on me & kept me under water for a short time. We each soon made the bank & continued our pursuit & after a mile hard gallop I headed & turned them home – having no saddle I galloped the horses back.

I returned to Boort on 7th. & commenced carrying & stacking my hay. The weather is now getting very warm & mosquitoes so bad that I am forced to burn dry cow-dung in my hut to smoke them out. I have lately shifted my sheep to an outstation 10 miles away where there is a fine lake of water known as Lake Leāghur – it is about a mile & a half long by three-quarter mile wide – this is for Australia a fine sheet of water. Here an intruder has had the impudence to put a fence round our hut, put in some wheat & turn the building into a stable. He is a neighbour & a Scotchman (of course) for they are invariably found to be here the most grasping & greedy of all settlers. I rode down there when I heard of it & spoke to him in pretty plain English & let him know that my sheep should shortly be there & show him whose property the hut and adjacent country was. The whole of settlers' quarrels with their neighbours is about country now, since it is getting very scarce. I consider myself now a fair distance from Melbourne (140 miles) considering others have to push out so much farther lately.

On the 18th. Dec. my wheat harvest commenced, but the crop has proved an entire failure owing partly to having been sown too late. There is very little for the sickle, the rest I shall mow for my horses – fowls or anything – as for another twelvemonth we must cart up our wheat from Melbourne.

24th. Still occupied with our wheat – I fetched in yesterday a bullock for killing at Xmas, having had a ride of 36 miles for him. It would surprise some at home to hear of riding as far as Teignmouth and back & driving a bullock or two before one – they are very contrary sometimes & charge the horseman, giving great trouble. We have killed 16 bullocks in the past year for station use.

Dear Margie's birthday was not forgotten by me. I pledged her in a hot tumbler of Whiskey.

Christmas day is a very warm one, spent by me in solitude, reading &

writing this. It is the first day I have spent at Boort without taking off my slippers – being indoors all day. I had a capital dinner of roast duck, green peas & young potatoes (our first garden produce) and a good plum pudding made by a person who has temporarily begged the shelter of my roof – hospitality knows no bounds in the Bush of Australia. He has been a fortnight here and makes himself generally available.

On the 8th. Jany. Dunsford & self left his station and got into Melbourne the following day riding 75 miles one day & 52 the next – not bad work.

I received an English letter from Maria dated Augt. 11th. from Canon Bridge.

[The conclusion of this letter is missing.]

The last of the letters which have survived was written two and a half years later, in May 1849. By that time Frederic had joined Henry at Boort and some of the responsibility for running the vast area of land with its increasing numbers of livestock was shared by the overseer, McWhirter – evidently a Scotsman of whom Henry approved – though the difficulty of obtaining employees meant that much of the routine work fell to those in charge, not that Henry was the least afraid of hard outdoor work.

In this letter to his mother there is the first hint that her second son, then aged twenty-five, was considering the possibility of marriage, something he had scorned a few years earlier, though he must have realised there would be little or no chance for him to meet a girl considered suitable to be his wife so long as he remained in Australia where women were still in short supply. He was delighted to see his cousin Augusta happily married and rearing a family at Mount Ridley some thirty miles north-west of Melbourne, her distress over the broken engagement to Mr. Vivian long since forgotten.

He reassures his mother there was no reason for her to worry about him being in danger from the local natives after she had read his detailed account describing some of the Aboriginal customs – their savage ways as yet uninfluenced by the intervention of white men. It is a pity he did not enlarge further upon the facts that he implied were known to him concerning the native habits and culture.

He makes some scathing remarks about the ex-convicts recently deported from Britain whom he compares unfavourably with the original law-breakers shipped out to the new continent earlier in the century, often for the most trivial of offences, many of whom, after serving their time, eventually became hard-working respectable citizens.

This letter takes the form of a diary, as do several of the others, but in this instance it is something which provides added interest because the journal kept by Frederic from 11th. May 1849 until the end of July 1853 overlaps some of the same period. Fred's journals were edited by his daughter Lillias Drought and published in book form in 1926; it can be seen that some of the earlier entries correspond with Henry's, and we can read about the same events described through the eyes of both brothers, in some cases the emphasis differing quite considerably.

Henry relates how he was disturbed after dark at about ten o'clock in the evening on 12th. May by the barking of his dogs, an indication that strangers were in the vicinity. The disturbance was explained by the arrival of Fred, back from a neighbouring settlement, together with Wilfred Sanger, an explorer of north-western Victoria in former days – in Henry's opinion a reformed character since their previous meeting because he had recently become a religious convert. Frederic, in his account, estimates their arrival at the homestead to have been about nine o'clock with the inhabitants then on the point of going to bed, but they were warmly received and were given a meal before retiring for the night. On the way to Boort from the Serpentine station Sanger and his companion had been delayed by a crowd of natives who were overjoyed at seeing the explorer again after an absence of three years, having presumed him to be dead. The "lubras" set up a noisy clamour of screaming and crying which was their way of signifying their pleasure – much to Fred's amusement.

The two versions describing the incident of the bucking horse differ quite markedly. As might be expected, Frederic relates it in a distinctly lower key because it was unlikely he would have joined in the laughter at his own expense. He simply says his horse Pestal began to buck when Henry mounted him, so he, Frederic, took over and rode away quietly. Only when in the paddock did he give him a cut with the whip which caused him to buck and send his rider flying over his head. No mention is made of his scornful remark to Henry that had triggered off the incident. On the whole, however, the brothers seem always to have had a very warm and close relationship. Of the two, Henry was the one who sometimes enjoyed playing the fool – as on the occasion of his twenty-fifth birthday celebrations at the Pearsons' home. Fred's young friend Lilly Chambers who was staying with the family at this time was the girl he had met on board ship three years earlier when she was fifteen and who was destined to become his wife in 1854.

On 28th. May, having received letters from home, Henry refers to the engagement of Maria to a certain H.P. The news seems to come as no surprise, though he implies that subsequently things had changed. Fred comments on his sister becoming engaged to H. Powell – whom we may assume was the son of the Mr. Powell who gave Henry his introduction to farming in South Wales. But Maria Godfrey did not marry the man in question. In 1850 the Reverend John Hill, Vicar of Welshpool, became her husband and in due course they had six children. It seems possible that she may have met him while staying with the Powells in Glamorgan – though this is, of course, pure speculation.

In the course of Henry's correspondence he mentions several occasions when he was obliged to spend many hours searching for his horses that had become lost in the Bush. In May, when writing to his mother, the quest to find "Quail" seemed to have been fruitless, thus we may conclude this horse was one of the many others to go astray in the days of the early settlers which founded the great herds of wild horses known today as brumbies that wander throughout the more remote regions of Australia.

No other letters exist, but a little more information can be gleaned by studying Frederic's journal up to the time the elder brother left for England in February 1850.

> Boort. Loddon River. Port Phillip
> May 18th. 1849

My dearest Mother,

I find myself now in the middle of August, sitting down to this epistle which was dated as above, left in my desk untouched for the last three months! Excuses are contemptible (because where there is a will, there's a way) and apologies at this distance needless, occupying space that may be devoted to more interesting matter; *ergo* at once my journal – but first slightly hinting that though I have been of late rather irregular, my English correspondents have somehow or other been affected in a similar way – animal magnetism, I presume, influencing people at the antipodes about the same time, and in like manner, though I trust not from a parallel cause. I have had no love affair to discompose my brain & agitate the system, hoping my turn will however *soon* come, and that you may all have an opportunity of witnessing it. I think my last was penned to Maria, posted the 24th. April, I having ridden to Johnson's Farm to post the letter, rested my oars at the Serpentine Station in the hopes of hiring some men to assist at the lambing of my sheep. On the 28th. April I drove Fred's horse "Pestal" in Tom Bear's spring cart to Boort, bringing with me our imported Box of Shirts &c. that arrived in Febry. last – You see although we get letters, or Boxes in Melbourne in a short time from home, many months frequently elapse ere they arrive at their final resting place, at some periods of the year the opportunities of carriage are many, at others very few. I believe in a former letter I thanked you kindly for the contents thereof, & am now able to give my unqualified approbation of the pattern & fit of the shirts, having worn then after a washing & the only thing I regret is the journal that fell to my lot (the lock-up Book) that I am expecting to fill it ere it will be possible to procure another, & I shall never again feel at liberty to write down so fully & frankly my thoughts & actions in any but a similar kind of Book. Now Fred's lock-up case on the other hand, can be filled with books unlimited. My days now (April) are passed in tending a flock, being quite unable to get men.

1st. May. Fred returned from the Serpentine bringing me a letter from Gus; in reply to which I thanked her for her uninteresting Bill of Ill health, for it teemed with accounts of sick husband, children & servants.

4th. May. Still sheep herding – and I find penned in my Book "What can be entered in a journal upon a day spent in heading sheep back, the refractory Ewes whenever they chose to roam on forbidden feed?" My amusement however, is derived from the perusal of the Books – generally the Protestant Magazine.

Sunday 6th. May. Seven black fellows arrived with their hair & faces thickly besmeared with mud, which is to them a mourning garb – the object of their grief was the death of Jacky, grandson of the King Jeribung – and heir apparent of the throne – certainly the best lad among the tribe for willingness to work & make himself useful. These 7 men were all day employed in breaking up glass bottles, small pieces of which are inserted & fixed with gum at the end of their long spears, which when complete is called "Micharro Koyune" & certainly an ugly weapon to find implanted in one's bosom, aye keener than Cupid's dart, and certainly more fatal. They tomorrow start for the Murray with death-bearing intent! for they return not amongst their own tribe until one, or more, of some other tribe by his life at their hands affords them satisfaction for their loss! They do not, when on this murderous mission, show themselves at any Station, or adhere to any beaten road, keeping themselves quite beyond the power of observation, when once their own district is traversed. They live in their wild state of olden times, getting of course no flour or tobacco. After, by cautious observation from the tops of high trees, they have from the smoke discovered the camps of the other blacks, they steal upon them in the darkness of night, & their deadly weapon is plunged into the sleeping, unoffending victims of their grief, or wrath. On chatting with them at night

& telling them how wicked & lawless was their design, and that white men never did so – they said "Never mind, always like it that Blackfellow." Happening moreover unwittingly to remark that I liked Jacky very much and meant to give him a shirt, it grieved me to see that I had touched upon a tender chord (not giving such savages credit for so great grief) they suddenly one and all set up a most hideous moaning and crying. And when it was over "Chalumin" begged me never again to mention aloud the name of the dead one and to tell Fred, or McWhirter to avoid the use of the name, because he was a great favourite. "Plenty like him that one all about blackfellow and big one cry." Their constant dread of Warrigal (wild) blacks taking some of them by surprise in expiation of their bereavement is, and will ever continue to be an insurmountable obstacle to securing their services as Shepherds or any other duty, which calls them out of the Bush beyond the sight or hail of habitations & whites. They willingly cut wood or fetch water about the home station, but will go on no errand unless you lend a "Yarraman" or "Gorgortarnook", either word signifying a horse. Only a few however of the young men are bold enough to venture as equestrians.

May 7th. Warm & sunny weather, relieved at last of shepherding, but only to be disgusted with the sight afforded at one of my outstations (where I rode) by the careless & shameful mal-treatment of my sheep by one of the invariably worthless set of *genus* "Pentovillain" who added impudence to injury – they may well be called "Lord Stanley's Pets", for without exception a greater set of accomplished rogues never came to these shores, far worse than the old convicts – for the education kindly bestowed on the former class, the care taken of them at Pentonville, Parkhurst & Millbank has been by them turned to bad account – accomplished, finished villains are worse than illiterate rogues – and these scamps are always ready to give a saucy answer and let you know that they are quite capable of teaching you the Law! The hardships endured by the old convicts served to teach them a lesson of civility which they have not forgotten, these educated pampered pets are a curse to the community – in the list of crimes & robberies committed in and about Melbourne the names of Pentonvillians figure in great majority. In fact I know there is a desire on the part of the youngsters generally to be convicted of some transportable crime or offence here because they feel themselves in a slighted position, scorned by all the old hands on account of never having gone through the severe ordeal of "lagging". If this paragraph were to appear in the Western Times anonymously I should have no objection for it would open the eyes of people at home to the folly of supporting such establishments as those mentioned.

8th. May. Drove a newly-hired man to take the place of the "Penton", for I got a fine volley of abuse; memo: in my journal was written – "Never again hire one of the sort at any price, if by the cut of his jib he is to be detected."

11th. May. The day on which Fred arrived at the so-called "years of discretion" was not marked by any peculiar incident or demonstration, as the hero of the day spent it at the Serpentine, from the untoward circumstance of my Pony "Quail" being astray, and Fred – a volunteer – seeking him. I was much interested in the perusal of Vincent Eyre's account of the sufferings of the British in Affghanistan – What a deplorable catalogue of disasters, dangers and sickness falling to the lot of British Ladies and the Army generally!

May 12th. A hard Day's work with my fast-increasing sheep. At about 10 p.m. was surprised by the barking of my Kangaroo Dogs, to give warning of the approach of visitors at this sequestered spot, and at such an hour! It was however fully accounted for in the arrival of Wilfred Sanger with Fred, the former making it a rule to travel by star light! Give me the sun's rays. To see the original discoverer & explorer of this Boort & Lower Lodden Country, and to give him my heartiest welcome afforded me great pleasure after an absence from Port Phillip of three years – but more especially was it delightful to observe the change wrought in him by the hand of God since his departure hence in April 1846, being now a religious man, whose constant companion is the Bible, its solemn & soul-saving truths forming the frequent and favourite topic of his conversation.

Sunday 13th. May. Sanger & I walked about Boort discussing & contrasting former days here with the present, talking of the changes that have taken place etc. Then at night after Fred & McWhirter went to bed we discussed Bible truths till 2 in the morning – so rare a thing it is to find anyone here who can take the least interest in things pertaining to God & Eternity.

14th. May. Fine days prevail succeeding frosty nights whereby the grass makes little growth. A very fatiguing day's work. Sanger proposed leaving, or rather had left, when finding me in a great fix with my men, very obligingly gave me his active and useful services all day, and but for his aid the flock could not have reached their destination, the alternative would have been a night in the Bush. For the evenings Fred & he fought at chess.

Tuesday 15th. May. Charley & two other blacks returned from their journey of expiation for the death of Jacky and in great secrecy the former told me he had mortally wounded a Black at Lake Boga in sight of two sheep station Huts – the victim was driving some horses for the whites when Charley speared him, but on account of the proximity of the huts he was unable fully to carry out his murderous purpose of finishing the wounded wretch with his "Seouwill" (a sort of club) and extracting the kidney fat! The fact of the poor wretch carrying with him a double-barrelled gun saved him from instant death; for though unable to run away, he "cooeyed" lustily for help and presented his piece at them, which succeeded in preventing them from running in upon him to complete the bloody task. I shall never again be incredulous respecting the sincerity of their fears at night, frequently expressed, about the approach of Warrigal Blacks since some of my own quietly-disposed tribe can visit a distant and hostile region to commit a cold-blooded murder. Why should not the Warrigals under the influence of a similar bereavement make also a death-seeking excursion into our district? All this minute detail, dear Mother, about the habits & customs of savages towards each other, need not at all alarm you on our account; I merely wrote it thinking it would be as interesting to you, at a distance, as it was to *me* on the spot. Moreover I might disclose facts in the history of these creatures probably not as yet brought under the observation of those who have written on the subject.

16th. May. Hearing tidings of the lost "Quail" I started for the Serpentine in quest of him.

17th. Tom Bear having lent me a horse I rode about 25 miles in every probable direction without success. Chatting & Chess playing formed the evening amusement of Tom Bear, Sanger & myself.

18th. May. Got the loan of another horse and scoured the neighbouring forests and plains, but no find. At midnight a heavy thunder storm & rain greeted our glad ears, we may shortly expect to see a fresh spring of grass for the poor sheep.

19th. May. Left the Serpentine & rode to Boort Station (27 miles.) My object in going there being to try & find my Chestnut Mare "Fairy" who has been running idly for the last 9 months in order to give a reprieve to my leg-weary filly "Zella," having been constantly ridden by me since I broke her in last September, scarcely fair play to a young and willing quadruped.

22nd. May. Boothe & his stockman brought me over a bullock for killing which was not downed till the third shot at his noddle: darkness having closed around the amateur Butchers (Fred, McWhirter & self) ere the beast was skinned and elevated on the gallows.

25th. May. Each day occupied in shifting the sheep to various stations where in the absence of water, good feed might be found. I started on Zela over to Boothe's, not having succeeded the other day in getting "Fairy", and passed the evening in the entertaining society of Mr. Boothe (a Butcher), his carpenter, stockman & hut-keeper! This is one of the rough stations in the Bush. What would Lord Chesterfield say about being forced to spend an evening in *such* company? I imagine "Suit yourself to it", fine words there would have been "pearls before swine" – so I regaled myself with a good meal and before a blazing log fire, with pipe blowing clouds of content, cared not a brass button who was on my right or left – a pretty comfortable shake-down (bed) however fully compensated for the disadvantages of an evening spent with boorish companions, at least sufferable for one night, and moreover there is some lesson to be learnt, beneficial to one, in every company.

26th. May. Got my mare into the stockyard, after some trouble put the bridle on her for she was very fat & *flash*, and then went to work with a chisel and mallet taking off some of her hoof which had grown to a great length, every one here his own farrier in an emergency. I then led her, riding Zela, to Boort where I found Fred busily engaged carting loads of earth for the formation of a Flower Garden.

27th. May. Left Boort on Fairy for the Serpentine. I took nearly all day riding the 18 miles, for my mare was too fat to be hurried. On my arrival there Sanger gave me a justly-merited reproof for riding on the Sabbath day – wilfully offending against a merciful God!

Mon. 28th. May. Before sunrise, in spite of a sharp white frost, rode to "Johnson's Inn" for my newspapers (having lately become a subscriber) and was rewarded for my *nipping* ride by receiving a letter from Augusta – and one for Fred from you, also a sheet from my dear Father to myself (date 30th. Dec. /48) with entreaties & persuasions for my visit to England not more earnestly expressed by him, than heartily desired by me, trusting to a good Providence for the speedy consummation of our reciprocal wishes. Maria's engagement to H.P. did not take me by surprise, but I will not recapitulate the entry made in my journal on the receipt of the intelligence, because circumstances have since been altered.

29th. May. Fine day after a sharp frost. Drove a shepherd to Boort to supply the place of a *bolter*. I have been caused more annoyance this year by the men than on any former occasion. We feel the absence of a Bench Magistrate in this district: and Government are so reluctant to grant the funds for so necessary an establishment, and we are the sufferers. The men know if they do wrong our redress is to be obtained by a ride of 90 miles to the nearest Bench! and 90 miles back! so it is more advisable to allow the guilty to go unpunished than undertake such a journey at the expence of the purse & inconvenience of the person.

30th. May. Got Fred's horse Pestal to ride the rest of the steeds into the Stockyards & he without provocation "bucked" most furiously – this you must know is a motion peculiar to Australian horses & *most difficult* to sit. Finding he could not throw me the horse stopped for a moment & Fred came out of the Hut with a half-laughing sneer of satisfactory scorn on his face, remarking, "Why Henry, you never got on any horse without making him restive & show off." So I immediately dismounted, saying "Well, as he is your horse, let me see whether it is altogether my fault & whether he will be ill-behaved with you, his master." – Wishing also that he should have an idea of the unpleasant sensation of sitting a "Buckjumper". He confidently mounted & scarcely was the horse many yards away before a cut of Fred's whip was only the forerunner of his turning a complete somersalt in the air, falling on his back! When I saw he was not hurt, it was a signal for a hearty laugh from me & those witnessing the scene – and my calling out, "Bring him here, Fred, for me to ride" put up his mettle, & he immediately remounted, taking care however not to ply his whip, and also to have him led away some distance by the bridle. I then rode Zela to the Serpentine on my way to Mt. Ridley, proposing for the first time since being in the Colony of going to court enjoyment of the kind offices & expression of good wishes of my only relatives here on my approaching Natal day – that is I went to spend the memorable 4th. June by special invite, with Augusta. Fred accompanied me to the Serpentine but for want of a horse in good condition for the journey, was unable to go on with me, saying he would be down by the 12th. June (Pearson's birthday). I reached Dunsford's Station by Saturday 2nd. June – but he, as usual during the courtship, was not at home. So I was entertained by his superintendant Mr. Bond, rested there the Sabbath.

Mon. 4th. June. I left Lancefield at daylight riding 15 miles in two hours to breakfast which was certainly rather a rough & ready sort of repast considering at least the residence there of a Mrs. Brock, not long since a Bride. I made a bold dash, worthy of this my birthday, to find a straight cut over and through all obstacles to Mount Ridley from Brocks'; but the sun suddenly and unkindly refusing me his aid & countenance left me in the lurch, and betrayed me to some fearfully steep rock gullies and ranges in crossing the "Deep Creek". It consequently took me 3 hrs. to get 12 miles! Memo: "The longest way round." &c. – and so it would have been for me; but on this day I felt game to attempt the most arduous undertaking. Reached Mnt. Ridley by 1 p.m. an almost unexpected guest, as my last letter held out scarcely any hopes of the probability of my coming down – it was however my private resolve (D.V.) to spend my 25th birthday with Gus, and with "nil desperandum" for my motto, all obstacles & difficulties were thrown aside. Found Fred's young friend and fellow passenger Lilly

Chambers on a visit, come to do honour to the day, as also Henry Pinson (of Dartmouth). After dinner we planted a number of young trees to form a shrubbery round the house – discussing a glass of sherry in drinking to the welfare of each tree planted on so propitious a Day. Even the little son & heir was made to grasp a tree, somebody also employed in holding him, while Pearson with a spade threw in the earth. The most difficult task was to disentangle the tree from his infantine grip, which is, you know, very tenacious. Though the day was cloudy I trust it was not ominous of my future career, but that the "Sun of Righteousness might arise" to disperse the clouds of sinfulness that have long overcast my dim sight to the danger of my eternal welfare.

The evening was of course joyously spent, as must always be the case, where so cheerful & kindhearted a person as Augusta is at the head of the merry-making – music & singing; and on this occasion I could not refuse to give them "I'm ninety-five" in real character – the old lady shewing her *agility* when the song was completed by standing on her head! – being a climax productive of roars of laughter at such an exposé – declaring to one and all they had never fallen in with so indecent an old Lady.

5th. June. Tremendous wind all day. I was made useful, not being an ornament, or rather as they required nothing ornamental for a stable, by polishing & cleaning a brace of silver-mounted pistols, an old family relic. A Mr. Furlonge spent the evening and Henry Pinson also extended his visit another day.

6th. June. A misty morning which turned to a cold raw rainy day wetting Pearson and myself through who had started for Melbourne in the Dog Cart. The roads of course in a miserable state. Pinson also left for Town *à cheval*. We did some business and then I dined and spent the evening with Mrs. Bear.

7th. June. Called on the Judge & one or two others, ordered a cart to be built & then left Town again by 2 p.m. with Pearson, having invited Ellen Bear and Miss Murchisson to Mt. Ridley on the 12th prox. (Pearson's birthday) volunteering to drive down & fetch them. We reached Mt. Ridley by dark after a good jolting.

8th. June. An English letter received for Maria for Fred about which I refrain from commenting, any more than it impressed me with a fit of melancholy all day.

9th. June. Pearson drove to Major Firebrace's, fetching sundry trees in his Dog Cart, which we all assisted to plant. I had for the first time for many months a good morning's violincello & piano playing. Lilly being the accompanist while Gus was attending to the important duties of her household.

Well, Mother, this is a strange medley of disconnected subjects, but I assure you 'tis the only form of letter that it is possible for me now to write, if uninteresting I cannot help it – suffice to say it is regular & minute, and as this is very closely written I will dispatch it as my June letter – hoping to pick up the thread of this last date in another to Emily to be shortly commenced. So with best love & kisses to my dear Father, sisters & Brothers & remembrances to all enquiring friends & relations, Believe me, ever your devoted & dutiful son

Harry Godfrey.

The original Godfrey homestead at Boort in 1862

6

Homeward Bound in 1850

On 15th. December the Godfreys together with McWhirter rode to what was known as the Remarkable Tree and thence along the top of the Kerang range until they came to a wide plain. On the way back they collected fuchsia seeds to plant in the garden. The next day Henry wrote a letter to Bishop Nixon. It is good to know he was still keeping in touch with that worthy man he had met five years earlier on the voyage out to Tasmania when he had no clear idea of what the future was likely to hold for him. Now he could report he was successfully established in his own sheep station and was happy in the way of life he had chosen.

Christmas Day 1849 saw the brothers once more at Mount Ridley. The day was passed in much jollity, playing the violin and with games of chess, while in the evening Henry – always ready to provoke laughter – dressed up in various disguises. The fun and games included the children and the servants in the kitchen.

On the second day of the new year, while still staying with the Pearsons, Henry and Fred rode over to the Bears' cottage and found poor Mrs. Bear in great pain after two sleepless nights owing to a badly sprained ankle. They then went to the Prince of Wales Hotel in Melbourne where a party was in progress. Henry, still in the mood to indulge in high jinks, caused much surprise and merriment by pretending to be tipsy. He had to be persuaded to come back after staggering halfway down the street, with the result they were not in bed until 4 a.m. Next day the brothers went on board the *Constance* – the sailing ship captained by John Bulwer Godfrey whose sister was the oft-mentioned "dear Gussie". Not until then was it disclosed that Henry's apparent drunkenness of the previous evening had been feigned – he had done it so well the others could hardly believe he had been shamming all the time. Then they spent a jolly day singing and toasting one another and the year just beginning, with the result that one of the party really did get "screwed" – as Fred put it. There was more gaiety on 7th. January when the brothers visited their friend Judge a'Beckett and afterwards went to a little theatre where plays and music were performed to an audience of about fifty people, most of them young. The evening ended with more comic songs from Henry. Three days later they attended a dance at which almost all the "aristocracy of Melbourne" were present.

They stayed at Mount Ridley until the middle of February while Henry was preparing to leave for England aboard the *Constance*. During much of this time he was suffering from severe inflammation of the eyes which forced him to wear a bandage and a blue veil. The weather was very hot and in the evenings they were plagued by flying insects of every sort and colour. On 12th. February they took part in another musical evening and Henry sang "The Blind Girl" in his fine tenor voice. The next day Frederic helped him to arrange his possessions aboard ship, filling the chest-of-drawers with his clothes and fastening everything down securely. They both slept on the ship and James Pearson was there, too. He had to get the cabin ready for his little daughter Janet who, with her nurse, was being taken to stay with her grandparents in Dartmouth in the care of her uncle, the ship's Captain.

They came ashore early on the 14th. and settled all business matters in town. That day they were invited to dine with Judge a'Beckett, but Henry's eyes were still so painful and disfiguring that he refused to go and Fred was only too willing to stay with him on their last day together. That night Henry slept at the Bears' cottage, while Frederic was at the Prince of Wales hotel. All passengers were expected to be aboard the *Constance* by four o'clock on 15th. February. The brothers drove down to the wharf and then went on a steamer crowded with passengers and the friends who were seeing them off. Once on board there was a lot of speech-making, drinking of toasts and singing sentimental songs, some people making fools of themselves by becoming tipsy and delivering hour-long speeches. Henry did not participate; he wrote letters in his cabin. That night Frederic slept aboard another ship docked in the harbour, but he had a very bad night suffering from a violent headache and feeling very depressed at the prospect of Henry's imminent departure. He remarked in his diary, "Dear Henry's kindness can never be forgotten by me." He knew that from now on all the responsibility of running the sheep station at Boort lay on his shoulders alone until such time as Henry should return – and as things turned out that was to be more than three years thence. Fred was only twenty-two.

He expected the *Constance* would have set sail and departed early the following morning, but at daybreak he was surprised to see she had not yet got under weigh and he learnt that two sailors had absconded the previous night, thus it was not possible for the ship to leave until replacements had been found. Luckily two other men on shore were willing to go at a moment's notice on the long haul back to the northern hemisphere. The final farewells were said as the ship prepared to weigh anchor. Little Janet

Pearson did not seem the least bit troubled at parting from her father; she was happy and excited at the prospect of the great adventure ahead of her. Fred watched the *Constance* sail away at ten o'clock with the royals set, forging ahead in a stiff breeze from the north at about eight knots. He returned to Melbourne with a heavy heart.

Soon afterwards he received a letter Henry had written hurriedly on board within hours of his departure. In it he said how their father had given him £1,500 to enable him to set up on his own in Australia and he had expected Fred to have received an equivalent sum on joining him at Boort. As he now knew this was not the case, presumably due to an oversight or some other reason, he felt it his duty to make up the difference to his younger brother now that he was being left in sole charge of the station. Therefore he wished to make over to him a quarter share of the Boort Station entirely for himself, plus the use of half of it for grazing speculations just as it might please him. In addition he would give him one thousand ewes. He hoped this would equalise their position and meet with their father's approval. Then he went on to advise Fred to keep strict accounts, following the example he had set, and he ended by apologising for the hasty scribble which was due to the accumulation of cares at the last moment and to the suffering caused by his eye trouble. In a postscript he exhorted his brother to keep the body occupied and to occupy the mind with religious thoughts, thus preventing discontent or despondency. He finished on an optimistic note: "We shall both do well, though it may be some time in coming." He signed himself "Harry".

The Godfrey brothers did do well and their success was not slow in coming. As it happened their ultimate prosperity was not due to sheep farming alone, though they certainly did that in a big way. Frederic reported eleven thousand and forty-one sheep were shorn on the station in 1852. Like many contemporary settlers they also took advantage of the boom in gold, mine workings having recently opened at Balarat and Bendigo. Fred in his journal made several references to calling at Bendigo, which lay on the route to Melbourne, and seeing great quantities of the precious metal in its raw state at the diggings. He bought samples which he sent to the city to be assayed. On 7th. September 1852 he mentioned that his father had sent him a bill of exchange to the value of £4,000 for him to invest in gold and promised a further £8,000 when Henry returned. These were vast sums at that time and they indicate Col. J.R. Godfrey must have been a very wealthy man.

For Henry the voyage home was not without interest. In March when they were sailing well beyond the coast of the Australian continent in the turbulent waters of the great southern ocean which washed its shores, an enormous iceberg was sighted. It towered like a mountain above smaller jagged fragments of ice, its slanting facets catching the sunlight and gleaming with the brilliance of diamonds, while the vast bulk that was in shadow assumed the hue of sapphires and emeralds. Henry did a sketch from the deck as the *Constance* passed quite uncomfortably close to the giant iceberg. Upon his return home an artist friend of the family by the name of Dutton used this sketch as the basis for a fine oil painting showing the barque in full sail forging ahead through heaving green seas fringed with plumes of spray and the great iceberg looming ominously in the background.

The barque "Constance" in which Henry Godfrey returned home to England from Australia for the first time in 1950. This painting was commissioned by his cousin, John Godfrey, the ship's Captain, and was given to him for his birthday some years later.

The picture was given to Henry on his birthday by his cousin John Bulwer Godfrey, Captain of the ship. Particulars of its origin are written on the back in Henry Godfrey's handwriting: "This Barque 'Constance' commanded by Capt. J. Bulwer Godfrey was the first ship sailed on the 'Great Circle' principle in 1849 to Adelaide, making the quickest voyage ever made of 77 days! H. Godfrey sailed to England on her return voyage from Melbourne when the iceberg was sketched by him in March 1850 and painted in by Dutton, the artist. The picture was given to me by Bulwer on my birthday to be an Heirloom. He died July 3rd 1881, buried at Dartmouth – Townstal church. H.G."

Henry himself was to die the following year.

7

The Later Years

Henry Godfrey arrived back in Plymouth on 29th. May after a hundred and two days aboard his cousin's sailing ship. There is no record of how he was occupied from that date until his marriage three years later, nor do we know when he became engaged to Mary Polwhele. They were married in Cornwall at St. Clements near Truro on 12th. May 1853. The bride was described on the marriage certificate as a minor, her age then being only eighteen, while Henry's profession was simply given as Gentleman. Preparations for their departure for Australia must have been made well in advance of the wedding because they left Exeter in June and sailed from Southampton on 14th. July, reaching Melbourne eighty-one days later on 3rd. October 1853.

This marriage was to link the past with the remembered present. Although Henry died in the nineteenth century, his wife survived him by almost fifty years and to her great-grandchildren Mary Godfrey was a significant figure in their childhood, while their memory of her lives on after a further sixty years.

When Mary realised she was pregnant she must have felt apprehensive at being in such a remote spot in a strange land on the other side of the world, deprived of all the home comforts she had taken for granted, thus her overriding desire was to return to England so that her baby might be born in familiar surroundings. Henry must have understood her feelings because he did not hesitate to make the long sea voyage again though it was less than six months since he had returned to the Boort homestead. He knew the station was in reliable hands and that Frederic was shortly to marry Lillias Chambers, the girl he had known and loved for the past seven years, so he and Mary left Melbourne on 26th. January 1854 and landed at Folkestone on 27th. April. Their first son, Henry Polwhele, was born in Exeter on 17th. May. The following year the birth of their second son, Clarence Polwhele, also took place in Exeter where the young couple were presumably staying with Colonel John Godfrey and his wife Jane Octavia who had moved from the old home at 5 Pennsylvania Park and were now living at Northernhay House.

Meanwhile in the summer of 1854 Henry had joined the South Devon Militia and was appointed as Ensign to serve with the Second Regiment of Militia stationed at Plymouth in the year made famous by the Crimean War. In August he was promoted to the rank of Lieutenant. Two battered parchment certificates exist authorising these appointments, signed by Hugh Fortesque, Lord Lieutenant in the County of Devon.

Life during this period could hardly have been more different from the mode of existence to which Henry had become accustomed in the Australian outback, and in spite of the proximity of family and friends he probably felt some nostalgic desire to return to the wooden house close to the lake which was now the focal point of the successful Boort Sheep Station. As Mary had seen the place, she now knew what to expect and, being several years older than when she first went there, she was developing the determination which was to be a feature of her character throughout her long life and so she was better prepared to meet possible hardships and difficulties with fortitude than when she was a young bride. This time, although she knew another baby was on the way, she was willing to accompany her husband on the long sea voyage and face the prospect of giving birth far away from home.

The decision to leave eleven-month-old Clarence behind with his Cornish grandparents at Helston must have been a hard one for the young mother to take. She probably thought it would be too risky taking such a small child on a long voyage at the age when he would be starting to investigate his surroundings and would need constant supervision. In the event of illness or accident there would be only the ship's doctor to turn to. The food, also, could present problems as there would be no means of obtaining fresh supplies until Cape Town was reached. The elder son, Polwhele, was still only two years and three months old, so Mary would have her hands full once the new baby was born, even though she doubtless had a nursemaid accompanying her on the voyage who would remain as a member of the household when their destination was reached. As it happened little Clarence was not to see his parents again for eight years and by that time they would have been complete strangers to him, so it must have been hard for the child to adapt to family life with two brothers whom he did not know.

Probably Mary suffered a certain amount of nutritional deprivation during the months she spent at sea before the birth of her third son, but there is no telling if this really was the cause of him being a puny infant and later a slightly built man of small stature, as he liked to claim. The voyage lasted ninety-five days and Ernest William was born eight weeks after his parents had landed in Victoria – at 10.10 a.m. on 28th. December 1856 at Cleveland House, Melbourne. The family must have stayed in the city pending the birth before they faced the long trek inland by horse-drawn carriage all the way to Boort. Here it was that Ernest spent the first eight years of his life – a life which, in spite of periods of delicate health, was to last for eighty-five years, until 1942.

The homestead at Boort – a single-story building surrounded by a wide verandah – was roomy and comfortable. Mary must certainly have had servants to do the cooking and perform the menial tasks, so she only needed to organise the smooth running of the household. Life there, though simple, was not now nearly as primitive as when Henry first came to live in Australia. A photograph of the house taken in 1862 shows the owner standing nonchalantly beside a post supporting the verandah, one leg crossing the other, while he appears to be in conversation with one of his small sons mounted on a pony. His wife is seated beside him, her wide crinoline skirt spread out decorously to conceal her ankles. The second child holds the bridle of another pony beside a wattle fence. A lower extension of the main building juts out on the far right-hand side, probably the kitchen or the servants' quarters. In the foreground lie two great trunks denuded of branches indicating that the area had earlier been cleared of gum trees and other vegetation in order that the house might be built there. The first wool shed was erected a mile to the south-east of the main dwelling and here in due course church services came to be held. On one occasion the shearers went on strike when they ran out of rum and tobacco, refusing to resume work until fresh supplies had been brought by dray from Melbourne. The wool was transported in these vehicles to the city and on the return trip food and other necessities were brought back. There were cattle yards half a mile from the homestead and a creamery near by. Here milk was brought to be separated, the skimmed milk being used to feed the animals.

The original little weatherboard house where Henry had first lived was now known as the bachelors' quarters. Here dwelt the farm manager, Mr. McWhirter, a huge powerful man whose great strength stood him in good stead when he succeeded in holding the door single-handed against two bush-rangers who were trying to force an entry with villainous intent, and he kept them at bay until help arrived. Stables, a carpenter's shop and another large wool shed now stood not far from the homestead.

The Godfrey brothers were responsible for creating an extensive lake from the swamp to the south of the hill on which the Aborigines made their smoke signals. A weir was built in the Loddon river and a canal dug a quarter of a mile in length with the help of native labour. The water from the river was thus diverted into the Keningapanule Creek which continued to flow into the swamp and flooded part of the surrounding land, consequently drowning a considerable number of trees. The lake thus formed was nearly two miles long and half that distance in width. At the mouth of the creek where it entered the lake a double row of posts was erected to form a sheep wash into which the sheep were driven before being shorn.

On their return to Australia Henry and Mary settled down at Boort with their two little boys. The sheep station was now a flourishing concern. Within two years the family was further increased by the arrival of another son. Prior to her confinement Mary had been taken to stay with the Pearsons at Mount Ridley and the baby was born there on 18th. November 1858. He was christened George Bertram. But tragedy struck when this latest arrival was only seventeen months old. The little child died on 11th. April 1860. The cause of his death has not been recorded. Was it due to an accident or was life in the outback a contributory factor? Of course we shall never know, though we do know the death occurred at the house of a Mr. Foote at Salisbury Plains in the Loddon District. Could this have been the home of a medical man whose help had been sought? Again we have no means of telling. At any rate the baby was buried there two days later and the grieving parents returned to Boort soon afterwards. Not liking to think of their child's remains lying so far away, they had the little coffin exhumed and re-interred at Boort on 5th. May 1860. The spot chosen for a cemetery was beyond the immediate precincts of the homestead on level ground close to the lapping waters of the lake, though above the reach of possible floods. Little Bertram Godfrey's grave was not the only one there. Two other headstones were already in position when his memorial was added.

Nine years previously a double tragedy had occurred on the night of 31st. May 1851. Frederic was then in sole charge of the station as Henry was in England. At the end of the previous year a young man by the name of John Campion had come out from Exeter to Boort in order to gain experience of life in the outback and to assist at the station, almost certainly at Henry's instigation. Fred mentioned him many times in the pages of his journal and he was evidently a willing worker who was a great help to have about the place, often accompanying Fred when rounding up or moving the sheep and cattle, and also assisting with other jobs such as shifting heavy equipment and painting the doors and window-frames of the house. Fred had spent the greater part of May in Melbourne on business and at Mount Ridley staying with his cousins. When he returned home on the 26th. after a very wet ride he found Campion gravely ill with what turned out to be dysentry. Next day the doctor was summoned and after the patient had been given some

The grave of Henry and Mary Godfrey's fourth son beside the lake at Boort.

medicine there seemed to be an improvement in his condition. But by the evening of the 30th. he became much worse and although every possible remedy was tried he continued to deteriorate. Fred and the doctor sat with him throughout the night and he died at half-past four in the morning.

In the evening of that same day Frederic heard that the six-week-old baby son of John and Jane who worked on the farm had also died. Thus two graves had to be dug side by side and the Burial Service was read over them. Other graves were to join these two and that of Henry's little boy as the years went on, one of them being an infant twin son of George Suttie who farmed in the Lower Loddon district while the Godfreys were at Boort. The surviving twin lived to be ninety-one. Not until much later was the first church built in the old Boort township that had grown up not far from the Godfrey homestead; it was constructed wholly of timber.

Near the sheep yards and the old wool shed where religious services were originally held there was the burial place of the Aboriginal king and queen, known respectively as Billy and Jerribug, who headed the Loddon tribe while the Godfreys were in residence. During excavations behind the homestead itself, an unidentified body was unearthed which was thought to be the victim of a native feud. The remains were covered up again and left undisturbed as the spot was thought to have an unpleasantly eerie atmosphere.

The Godfrey family and their workers on the station had a good relationship with the local Aborigines who were employed to cut wood, fetch water and carry messages. Life for the two little boys, Polwhele and Ernest, was full of interest and excitement. The natives taught them how to catch crayfish in the creek, to dig for yams and other edible roots and to find opossums hiding in the trees. They were told about the occasion when Charley, normally an affable and docile blackfellow, had smeared himself with mud and set off together with a companion on a mission of revenge. They speared their enemy, but were prevented from killing him. Ernest was always to remember the day he went into the carpentry shed to watch the men at work sawing and planing the wood, when he happened to look down and saw the shavings on the ground near his feet heaving and quivering. A huge mottled snake emerged and glided towards a dark corner under the bench, but it was quickly dispatched by one of the men wielding an axe.

In 1863 Henry and Frederic sold their Station at Boort to Dr. Robert Farie. By this time a small township was growing up beyond the environs of the original homestead. There was a resident blacksmith, a hostelry, a saddler and a general merchant. On leaving Boort Henry purchased the Nangunia Station in New South Wales, and after appointing a manager to take charge there, he left Australia in the following year with his family to settle near Cheltenham where he bought a house he called Karenza, a Cornish name favoured by his wife. Frederic remained in Australia for the rest of his life and some of his descendants live there at this present time.

After their return to England another son was born to Henry and Mary. Charles Montagu Bell (subsequently known in the family as Monty) made his appearance on 29th. April 1865. The Godfreys were now able to live in an opulent style, Henry having done well for himself during the twenty-one years since he had left home as a lad of nineteen. He did not, however, live to enjoy his good fortune into a ripe old age. Towards the end of his life he was plagued by gout and he died at Queen's Gate in London at the comparatively early age of fifty-eight on 8th. May 1882. He was buried at Leckhampton, the village on the outskirts of Cheltenham where his home was. Many gentleman from the town were present at the funeral and in a contemporary newspaper it was recorded the deceased was a highly respected member of the Freemasons' Lodge as well as having been a local Magistrate. The blinds were drawn down in many of the shops and in the private residences overlooking the route along which the funeral cortège passed. The coffin was piled high with wreaths of white flowers, a particularly beautiful tribute being placed there by the members of St. Luke's church choir. The Reverend J.A. Aston, who officiated at the grave, appeared to be deeply affected. Henry Godfrey had clearly been held in high estimation by all who had known him.

8

Bridging the Gap

In deciphering and studying the faded letters written so long ago by Henry Godfrey along with the information concerning him contained in various family records, he emerges as quite a different character from the stern individual he appeared to be as portrayed in photographs and in the portrait of him painted in his middle years. In his youth at any rate he seems to have been a person with a real sense of fun who was not averse to playing the occasional practical joke or even making a downright fool of himself for the amusement of others. He was a talented musician gifted with a beautiful singing voice, a competent draughtsman, a hard worker not afraid of arduous physical labour in the most unpropitious conditions, and an excellent horseman. A man plainly with great determination and plenty of practical good sense, he was generous and thoughtful, devoted to his parents and to all his family connections. The continual emphasis he placed on his religious faith may seem over-stressed, making him appear a pious prig by modern standards, but of course it was simply the expression of the type of upbringing he had had, which was common in the majority of well-to-do Victorian households. Anyhow, it is clear his religious beliefs meant a great deal to him, supporting him when circumstances were difficult, and he was not afraid to give voice to them in the face of critical opposition. He must have been a good business man, too, keeping strict accounts and recording full details of all transactions connected with his sheep station. He lived at a time when every educated person was a good correspondent and he also kept a daily journal, though only one small diary of his has survived from the years he lived at Boort. However, the letters he wrote were largely in the form of a diary.

To Henry Godfrey's great-granddaughters the name of Boort has been familiar since childhood. We knew our grandfather Ernest had spent the first eight years of his life there and he continued to correspond with relatives in Australia well into his old age. None now remained in Boort itself, but there were some members of the family in other parts of Victoria, principally around Melbourne. Frederic's descendents were still in Australia; William had emigrated there in 1857; and the son of their youngest brother Charles, also named Charles, had arrived at Port Phillip in 1883 to become a bank manager at Portarlington, in Victoria. I was put in touch with his granddaughter Mildred Godfrey as we were much the same age; we wrote to one another intermittently over the years, though I had no reason to think it would ever be possible for us to meet.

My parents had written to members of the Historical Society in Boort so as to forge a link with the town that had grown up in the place where our ancestor had been the pioneer settler, and during the War we received very welcome food parcels sent by the kind people of the township to augment the meagre rations we were allotted in Britain at that time. Many years later my sister's husband made typewritten copies of the letters Henry Godfrey had written from Australia and extracts were published in the *Boort Standard* newspaper during the summer of 1980.

The motivation for making transcripts of my great-grandfather's letters and finding out more about him did not occur until I had attained the status of a grandmother and a senior citizen, and then it was triggered off – in part at any rate – by circumstances leading to an event I had never dreamed possible. The prospect of actually visiting the place where my great-grandparents had lived in far distant Victoria had not at any time entered my head. For one thing I had an almost pathological fear of flying and swore nothing would ever induce me to travel by air, and for another I knew such a journey would entail considerable expense which was beyond my means.

But after my step-son had been living in Australia for several years, my husband and I began to consider the possibility of going out there to see him even though this would mean I would have to overcome my phobia. I wrote to my cousin Mildred and also to the Secretary of the Boort Historical Society to say we were thinking of visiting Australia in the spring of 1988 and if this idea materialised we would of course like to meet my relatives out there and see the spot where my ancestors had lived during the middle of the previous century. But it seemed as if our plans were to be dashed when my husband had a 'phone call from his son at Christmas time to say he was coming home in March, just when we had proposed going to visit him, so of course there would be no object in our making the journey. When I informed Mildred of this she wrote back promptly urging me "to take the plunge" and come on my own. She added that I would be very welcome to stay with her and her husband near Melbourne and in the course of my stay they would make a point of taking me to Boort. Knowing I might never get another similar chance, the temptation was too strong to resist and I went ahead with preparations for what I felt certain would prove to be one of the most interesting experiences of my life.

The flight to Australia took twenty-four hours, the plane touching down only at Bangkok. I thought of the times my great-grandfather had travelled by sailing ship to the other side of the world, the sea voyages then lasting at least three months. To make the journey in so short a time, let alone to come by air, was something he could never have envisaged in the wildest stretch of imagination.

After spending a week with friends near Sydney in New South Wales I flew on to Melbourne and was met at the airport there by Mildred and Ivor Buchanan who drove me to their delightful bungalow some twelve miles from the outskirts of the city. While staying there I met other members of the Godfrey family descended from Henry's youngest brother Charles, an uncle of my grandfather's.

Then came the day when we set out at eight o'clock in the morning to drive about a hundred and fifty miles from Diamond Creek to Boort in the north-west of Victoria. Once we got clear of the populated areas the roads led onwards dead straight across level and rather featureless country, the grasslands parched in the March sunshine and scattered with isolated gum trees which provided pools of shade for the groups of sheep and cattle sheltering beneath them. For the greater part of the way the road was wide, the central portion being tar-macadamed while on either side it was unsurfaced. There was very little traffic, thus on few occasions was the dust disturbed by a passing car. But this did not apply all the time. There were sections of the road that were not surfaced at all and then a cloud of red dust was seen to presage the approach of an oncoming vehicle. When the two cars passed both were enveloped in a haze of dirt momentarily dimming the sunlight. Of course in the days of the first settlers there were no straight roads and the country had not been cleared of bush. They made their way along uncharted tracks on horseback and with heavy drays transporting their goods, encountering clouds of red dust in dry weather, while when it rained the route was turned into a morass of mud.

We passed through the pleasant town of Bendigo with its mine workings where fortunes of gold had been made in the middle years of the last century and even today the workings showed some signs of activity. At Durham Ox we took the left-hand fork at the crossroads where Boort was signposted. Here a life-size cut-out replica of an enormous bull was suspended outside a building at the road junction. The Durham breed of cattle had been introduced into this region by Edward Argyle who came to Australia about the same time as Henry Godfrey and who in addition to cattle, bred horses branded with the letters OX – hence the name adopted for the settlement he and a man called Boothe developed at this spot. In the opposite direction to the road that we took, the signpost indicated the way led to Pyramid Hill.

It was mid-day when we reached Boort, having travelled the distance in four hours that used to take Henry Godfrey and his brother at least three days on horseback. I had seen photographs of the town sent to my parents and grand-parents in the course of the past fifty years, so I had some idea what to expect. The present town grew up at the opposite end of the lake to where the original homestead was, but its joint founders are commemorated by the main street being named after them. It is called Godfrey Street. To see the name jutting out from a post where the wide road forked at the head of the lake gave me a singular thrill. To have come so far and see tangible evidence of my own connection with this place was ample reward for travelling half way round the world. All the main buildings are situated in this street. Here are the shops, the post office, various offices and municipal buildings and the old Court House, now housing a museum where the Historical Society hold their meetings. At the far end of the town stands the imposing Railway Hotel, though now no passenger trains stop at the station, the railway being used for goods transport only. Near the head of the pretty tree-bordered lake there is a bowling green, a caravan site and a swimming pool. It was here, at the start of Godfrey Street, that we turned off to find the charming bungalow home of Mrs. Freda Fawcett, the Historical Society's secretary. A stone's throw from the front garden across the dusty road lay the calm blue water of the lake where ducks and birds resembling moorhens dived and dabbled close to the reed-fringed shore.

We received a warm welcome from Mrs. Fawcett who introduced us to Mr. Bob McMillan and Mr. Robert Coutts, members of the Society and residents of Boort who could claim descent from early settlers. We were given a sumptuous meal in the beautiful spacious bungalow with antique furnishings and original paintings on the walls. Afterwards the six of us drove off in two cars to see the spot where Henry and Mary Godfrey had lived in the mid-1850s and early '60s.

The route taken led us out of the town by the way we had entered it and after a mile or so we turned off towards the lower end of the lake. A track took us to a single-storey farmhouse now standing approximately where the Godfrey homestead used to be. Hens pecked about and scrabbled in the dust just as they had doubtless done all those years ago. On the edge of an area of trampled dry earth there stood a lopsided wooden shed which we were told dated from those early days, though it had since been moved from its original site to the position it now occupies. It looked now to be on the point of collapse. The galvanised roof had obviously been added at a later date to replace the timber one, but the supporting posts leaning at drunken angles and the weatherbeaten door appeared to be of great antiquity. Mildred and I stood within the gaping entrance to have our photo taken since we were representatives of the Godfrey family.

Then we were taken beyond the farmyard to see the little cemetery by the lakeside where weather-worn tombstones marked the resting places of those who had died prematurely over a hundred and thirty years before. There was the memorial to eighteen-year-old John Campion who never returned to tell his parents in Exeter about the new life he had found on that farm so far from home. The infant child of the farm worker John and his wife Jane was remembered on a stone close by, though their surname was not recorded. The grave was there of a child whose twin brother had lived to be over ninety, and in the centre a stone stood bearing the inscription "Sacred to the Memory of GEORGE BERTRAM Fourth son of Henry and Mary Godfrey. Born 18th. Nov. 1858. Died 11th. April 1860."

As I gazed at these words I felt my eyes moisten with tears. Here lay the remains of my dearly loved Grandpa's little brother born of the flesh and blood I had inherited who, had he lived, would have been a great-uncle of mine, someone I might have known. The place where these few rested seemed to me to have an atmosphere of timeless peace. Some twenty years earlier the members of the Boort Historical Society had undertaken the job of restoring the little graveyard after it had become overgrown with vegetation and the stones had fallen down or were broken. Now it is surrounded by a metal fence to keep out animals and the headstones have been cleaned, mended and re-erected. A slender gum tree towered above this little plot of earth containing forgotten tragedies known to so few.

Beyond the fringe of trees which cast a welcome band of shade on the parched ground, lay the lake. Its waters at this end were very low and an expanse of reddish soil pitted with the footprints of cattle extended for some distance beyond the bank. Our informative guides pointed out the remains of the Godfrey's sheep wash close to the spot where the creek entered the lake. A double row of dark posts, now reduced to rotting stumps like the decayed and blackened teeth of some prehistoric monster, showed where the sheep used to be penned to have their fleeces cleaned before shearing commenced. The wash had originally been six feet deep in the centre and some twenty feet in length. About a dozen animals were dealt with at a time by a number of men who stood waist-deep in the water beside the palings, rubbing and teasing the wool with their hands in order to loosen the grime. Soft soap and soda was worked into the fleeces and then rinsed out under a spray controlled by a pump. This left the wool snowy white. Today the water at the margin of the lake was shallow and discoloured with patches of floating scum, while the creek was stagnant and green with algae.

I felt the whole area here, tranquil in the blazing sunshine, held – for me at any rate – echoes of times long gone when two little boys played beside the swamp under the benign and watchful eye of their bearded father, while their mother, dressed in a crinoline frock so unsuited to the sort of life she was leading, sat in the shade beside the farmhouse door stitching away at the delicate embroidery she executed with such expertise, work with which she continued to pass her leisure moments throughout her long life. Yes, my grandfather and his mother, both of whom figured so significantly in my youth, had actually walked about in the place where I now was – both of them then, of course, so different from the way they had looked to me in my childhood – an old man and a still older woman in far distant Devonshire.

From the lakeside we were taken to a spot where two roads crossed. Standing on the grassy verge in a patch of shade cast by a group of trees which afforded welcome relief from the glaring sun, though not from the

The remains of the sheep-wash in Lake Boort close to the site of the original homestead.

hordes of flies incessantly plaguing us, we were told this was the site of the first township at Boort. Across the road there had once been a public house, while close by, two blacksmiths and a farrier had catered for the many horsemen in the district – for without horses there would have been no means of contact with the rest of the civilised world. Here, too, there was once a general store and a post office. No signs now remained of the buildings once comprising this little community. Most of them had been made of timber, while others were constructed in part of tin. By the late eighteen-seventies this old township had ceased to be viable and the new town was growing up at the northern end of the lake.

Today Boort is the prosperous centre of an agricultural area where the main industries are still the breeding of sheep and cattle for wool, meat and dairy produce together with grain production and the cultivation of lucerne for animal fodder.

The following morning I walked up the gentle slope leading to the summit of an eminence my Grandfather remembered being called Bald Hill, now bald no longer. Today a copse of trees crowns the point where the "blackfellows" once made their signalling fires. From here I could see the town below and the blue water of the lake that owed its existence to my great-grandfather and his brother. How gratified they would have been if they could have looked into the future and seen Boort as it was going to be towards the end of the twentieth century! Although the population is less than a thousand it struck me as being a remarkably complete and all-embracing little community. There is a hospital, a High School, splendid sports facilities, churches of several denominations, numerous clubs and other organizations catering for varied interests and activities.

For me the climax of my visit came on the second evening when I was honoured to be guest speaker at a meeting of the Boort Historical Society in the old Court House, now serving as a well-arranged museum where many relics from the past are on display.

It was an emotional moment for me when I was introduced to a packed audience seated on benches and on hard-backed chairs filling the hall. I said that not in my wildest dreams had I ever imagined I would actually visit this spot where my forebears had once lived far away in Australia. Having known my Great-grandma, Mary Godfrey, wife of Boort's pioneer settler, I felt the past was joined to the present although the time thus bridged amounted to well over a hundred years. I spoke of my early memories of my great-grandmother when she had lived in Exmouth as a very old lady, and then I went on to talk about the family in general. After saying I had at home a number of letters written by Henry Godfrey in the 1840s, I proceeded to read from a copy I had brought with me of the letter he wrote on Christmas Day 1846, pausing when I neared the passage dealing with the troublesome Scotsman. At this point I remarked I was afraid Henry had a very poor opinion of the Scots so I trusted anyone present of Scottish descent would not take offence. This was greeted with much laughter as it turned out that Mr. Bob McMillan – whom I had already met – the Society's President, was the great-grandson of the John McMillan with whom my great-grandfather had disputed over boundary and land rights. At any rate it was now possible to say any rift which might have existed between the families in the past was finally healed.

When my talk ended I was rather taken aback at being asked to pose for my photograph by a representative of the local newspaper, the *Boort Standard and Quambatook Times*. I stood on the dais at the back of the room pointing at an old picture fastened to the wall showing a group of Aborigines – a picture mentioned in a letter from my Grandfather who remembered the individuals illustrated there. The following week an article giving an account of my talk was published on the front page of the newspaper under the heading "How Short is our History!"

As I descended the steps from the stage at the end of the meeting I was surrounded by people asking questions, all so welcoming and friendly, all making me feel this was indeed one of the most memorable days of my life. On leaving Boort that evening to stay with Lindsay and Joyce McClelland at their farm near Lake Marmal some twelve miles away I was able to reiterate what my great-grandfather had written a hundred and forty-two years earlier: ". . . hospitality knows no bounds in the Bush of Australia."

8

The Past Revived: The Sketchbook

After my return from Australia I felt my experiences there, particularly at Boort, had helped to give me some insight into the sort of life my great-grandparents must have led during the time they lived there. At least now I could picture the type of country they had known, for although much had obviously changed out of all recognition in the course of the past 130 years or so, the topography of the region, its kind of vegetation and climate were still much as in those days. I had no reason to think, however, that Henry Godfrey was remembered or was considered to have been of interest to anyone outside our immediate family, nor that he had left anything of lasting value apart from the small collection of his letters I possessed and which I hoped would continue to be preserved along with other family archives by my descendants in the years to come. It was true I had seen his name mentioned in an account of Boort and its development displayed on a screen in Melbourne museum, but of course he was only one of a number of early settlers who had helped to colonise what is now known as the State of Victoria, and who had prospered there. This being so I was greatly astonished to receive a letter from a friend living in Melbourne shortly before the following Christmas asking me if I knew about the discovery of the sketchbook described in the newspaper article she was enclosing.

It was a half-page article entitled "Fragments of our History" from the Saturday Extra edition of *The Age* newspaper dated 22 October 1988 and it dealt with a sketchbook of Henry Godfrey's that had recently come to light. The paper had published colour reproductions of four of the pictures contained in the book. The account by Geoff Maslen told how a book of 130 sketches in pen and ink, pencil and watercolour done by Henry Godfrey between the years 1841 and 1863 had been discovered and was being offered for sale by the present owner for the colossal sum of thirty-five thousand Australian dollars (about £16,000 in our money at that time). The Victoria State Library was very anxious to obtain the book so that it might be preserved there for posterity as it was considered to be of great historical interest. Some of the pictures gave a unique impression of life in Australia

120

during the middle years of the last century and before, and they were thought to be among the earliest drawings of their kind to exist. The Library could not afford the sum asked, but hoped it could be raised by public donations. The article went on to describe in mainly accurate outline the life of Henry Godfrey and gave some interesting facts about the Aboriginal population at the time when he came to Boort as the first white settler.

Naturally I found all this absolutely fascinating. But I must admit my first reaction was to wonder why this sketchbook, now considered to be of such great value, had not been kept in the family. Why had my great-grandfather not brought it back with him when he had finally returned to England in 1864 and where had it been during all the years since then? It seems doubtful that I shall ever learn the answers to these questions. I am afraid I could not help feeling more than a little aggrieved that an item of such interest had not been passed down to Henry's direct descendants. If anyone was entitled to have the sketchbook surely I happened to be the one with the most valid claim – and my sons and their children after me? However I realised there was absolutely nothing I could do on that score, thus in the circumstances I hoped the State Library would procure the book so that henceforward it would be in permanent safe keeping.

My sister and I both wrote to the Librarian in Melbourne to ask for further particulars about the discovery of the sketchbook, but it seemed she was not prepared to disclose any more facts owing to being obliged to respect the anonymity of the person wishing to sell it, whose identity was evidently a confidential matter. This we found very frustrating because we should have liked to have been able to communicate with the individual concerned as the sketches were the work of our direct ancestor. We could only guess that either Henry had left the book with his brother Frederic or else he had given it to his eldest son, Henry Polwhele, who had returned to Australia in 1872 and died at St. Kilda near Melbourne in 1917, though some of his children had been born in New Zealand. It is possible the sketchbook may have belonged to one of them, but now I was back in England I had no means of tracing them or their descendants. Anyhow we were pleased to learn in due course that the Library was successful in raising the money required for the purchase of the sketches – though for me the story did not quite end there.

It so happened that my younger son, Brian Wilkinson, who is employed by the P & O Company as a Radio Officer on their container ships, was going to be in Melbourne in February 1989. I had met him there the previous April when his ship was in the harbour loading containers for the homeward-bound voyage and, as on that occasion, I knew he would have several days in port. Accordingly I wrote again to the Librarian asking if my son might call at the library and be allowed to see the sketches done by his great-great-grandfather which I understood were now the property of the State Library.

I waited impatiently for a letter from Brian telling me of his visit. When it eventually came I read that he had found the library staff exceedingly helpful as soon as he announced his identity and he was ushered into an inner sanctum of the Arts section where the sketchbook was produced for his inspection. It was removed from a plastic bag and he was presented with a pair of white cotton gloves to wear as he turned the pages. The book was small, only about seven inches by three-and-a-half, the leather covers battered and the binding splitting, but the pages were in good condition. Of the 167 leaves a few were blank and only fifty-six illustrated the Port Phillip district, though there were quite a number done on Henry's first voyage in 1843 depicting the approach to Cape Town and the views sketched during his week's stay there when the *Duke of Roxburgh* was anchored in Table Bay. One showed the ship itself. But the first forty-three drawings were of subjects in England, some executed as early as 1841 when he was only seventeen years old. These included views of Dartmouth, Exeter and Exmouth, and others showed places in Herefordshire, Westmorland and South Wales. There were also some studies of flowers, animals and trees. All these would have been of great interest to me, living as I do in the south-west of England, whereas they were unlikely to mean much to anyone in Melbourne. Brian was given a complete list of all the pictures as well as photocopies of some documentation relating to them and of information concerning the Godfrey family at Boort taken from a book dealing with the early pioneer families in Victoria. Most of the facts given must have been orginally obtained from the book compiled by Frederic's daughter Lillias Drought which includes the copious extracts from his journal I have already mentioned, so I did not learn anything new.

As Brian carefully turned the frail little pages he heard the librarian say to her assistant *sotto voce*, "Watch him!" Did they expect him to try and slip one or two of the loose pages into his pocket? Amused, but at the same time far from pleased by the inference, he nevertheless left the library feeling very proud his ancestor's handiwork should now be so highly valued. In his letter he reported the sketches were drawn with great delicacy and attention to detail which gave them a clarity and accuracy that was almost photographic in character. The naiveté of style, particularly where figures were concerned, tended to add to the spontaneity of the subjects rather than to emphasise their rather limited artistic merit. He could obtain no further information regarding where the book had come from except to be told it had "moved sideways in the family". This leads me to suspect it had been handed down by Frederic to one of his descendents, several of whom remained in Australia, a supposition born out by the fact that the last of the pictures was dated 1863, the year Henry left Boort.

It is unlikely I shall ever return to Australia and have the chance to see my great-grandfather's sketches for myself. Nevertheless it is some consolation that one of them must have been detached from the book and kept together with the collection of Henry's letters that were passed down in direct line to the present day through five generations. It is the little pen and ink drawing of Table Mountain with sailing ships moored in the Bay in the foreground, intricately drawn and shaded with a very fine nib and tinted with a light watercolour wash – one of the sketches of this subject he mentioned doing when he wrote home in May 1843.

I notice in the list supplied of the subjects in the sketchbook that the hundred and nineteenth page shows the iceberg sketched by Henry aboard the *Constance* in March 1850 which was copied by his artist friend Dutton when he incorporated it into his oil painting of the sailing ship – the picture which has happily come down to me and will be inherited by one of my sons as specified on the back of the frame.

Since learning that my great-grandfather is considered worthy of having a place in the history of Australia, both as the founder of the little town where the main street bears his name and because of the value attributed to his drawings illustrating those early days, I felt compelled to find out more about him for myself and get some idea of the kind of man he really was. I had always known of the existence of his letters kept in the heavy metal box we called the Family Box, but I had never taken the trouble to read them properly. Every attempt I made had been thwarted by the difficulty in deciphering the closely written handwriting with characteristics peculiar to the first part of the nineteenth century. Now, having an added incentive, I set to work systematically and persevered – my interest increasing as I progressed – until all were typed out legibly.

For me it was been a rewarding task and I hope others may also find these recorded facts of Henry Godfrey's life and the personality that has emerged of some interest.